The Manchester United
Football Book
No. 4

THE
MANCHESTER UNITED
FOOTBALL BOOK
No. 4

Edited by
DAVID MEEK

Foreword by
BOBBY CHARLTON, O.B.E.

STANLEY PAUL
London

STANLEY PAUL & CO LTD

178-202 Great Portland Street, London, W1

AN IMPRINT OF THE HUTCHINSON GROUP

London Melbourne Sydney
Auckland Bombay Toronto
Johannesburg New York

First published 1969

This book has been set in Plantin type face. It has been printed in Great Britain by Taylor Garnett Evans & Co. Ltd by offset lithography at Watford, Hertfordshire

09 097860 9

Contents

European Cup football means a fair amount of time spent waiting for planes in foreign airports . . . like this one on the Continent where editor David Meek and Bobby Charlton take time out for a glass of tea

Foreword

by

BOBBY CHARLTON, O.B.E.

(Manchester United Captain)

EVERYONE at Old Trafford knows that we face a tremendous challenge this season. We didn't do too well in the League last winter and though we had a good run to the semi-finals of the European Cup, we were all very disappointed to see this great trophy leave the club.

So we have some lost ground to make up and at the same time we are of course losing 'The Boss' as our immediate team chief. Sir Matt Busby is to become general manager while one of our former playing colleagues, Wilf McGuinness, takes over as chief coach.

No one can be sure just how this change-over will work out. After all Sir Matt has been at the helm of Manchester United for 23 years. He has been the boss in every sense of the word . . . manager, tactician, coach, adviser, disciplinarian, simply everything.

Even though he will be there in the background still, we are bound to miss him. But of one thing I am sure, United could not have chosen a better man to follow in his footsteps.

Some people seem to think that an ex team-mate could not command the necessary respect and authority. Well, it may not be easy, there will be problems, but what people outside forget is that football is a very competitive profession and that from the moment you come into it your friends are also your rivals.

Your best buddy may put you out of the team and you learn to accept sudden changes in fortune, just as we shall quickly accept Wilf McGuinness as 'Boss'. Don't forget, either, that Wilf has been on United's training staff for six years now and he is no stranger to putting the rest of us through the hoop!

Another man who sometimes puts us through a different kind of hoop is David Meek, the *Manchester Evening News* football writer who goes wherever Manchester United go.

This is his fourth book in what is now an annual close-up on the United scene. No one is in a better position to describe United's successes and disappointments and I am confident that like his earlier books, this one will also bring you closer to Old Trafford.

It's a link between us, the players, and you, the fans, to help provide a little soccer interest between matches. It is also becoming a permanent record of our fortunes which personally I find interesting to have. It is a pleasure to introduce The Manchester United Football Book No. 4.

Challenge for United's New Boss

WILF McGUINNESS, 31-year-old trainer of Manchester United's reserve team, is the man chosen to follow in the famous footsteps of Sir Matt Busby.

For three months the whole of football speculated on who would follow the great man, and mention of all the names proposed in that period would fill a book.

Yet though the qualities of many of the men suggested, like Burnley's Jimmy Adamson, spoke for themselves, there should be no surprise that the post has gone to a man already at Old Trafford.

Manchester United are that kind of club. All the senior staff appointments have come from within 'the family'. Jack Crompton the trainer and John Aston the coach were both players with United. Chief scout Joe Armstrong only took the full-time position after many years scouting on the road for the club. Even secretary Les Olive started at Old Trafford as a junior player.

So the man who joined United as a starry-eyed 15-year-old Manchester schools player now takes charge of some of the most talented even temperamental, certainly the biggest soccer stars in the game. He also has to try and match the most consistent record of success in post-war football, the legendary reign of Matt Busby.

It's a tough assignment, a frightening inheritance. Sir Matt is convinced his successor can do it. So too is Jimmy Murphy, United's assistant manager who watched the youthful McGuinness make the grade after being rated one of the most unlikely looking footballers to attract the attention of professional clubs.

As Jimmy Murphy says: 'I saw Wilf in schoolboy football and it would be impossible to imagine a more ungainly looking player. On his own admission he is flat-footed, knock-kneed, and ran with his knees up in a peculiar style.

'He reminded me somewhat of a young colt put out to grass for the first time.

'Yet, despite these apparent disadvantages, Wilf became a most successful footballer and played for England. All credit to him for overcoming these natural disadvantages.'

As a schoolboy for Manchester, Lancashire, and England, the young McGuinness had a number of clubs interested in him, and United were one of them. Eventually he was signed by Jimmy Murphy in the back of a car outside Manchester's fruit market, where Mr. McGuinness, senior, worked.

Says Murphy: 'Actually, it took us some time to sign him. Joe Armstrong met his parents and eventually I did as well, but we didn't seem to be getting anywhere.

'So much so that my patience became a little exhausted and I finally put the question to Wilf – are you joining us, yes or no?

'I also asked him if he thought he was Duncan Edwards, as we sat in the back of the car.

'You see, even in those days Wilf was a youngster who knew his own mind and was capable of expressing himself quite determinedly.

'When he eventually arrived we had a tremendous amount of work to do on him. My late friend Bert Whalley did a heck of a job with Wilf and he must never forget it.

'He developed into a player who was a prodigious worker. He was also a good listener. He never missed a trick, and even at the age of 15 was always seeking guidance and advice.

'It stood him in good stead and he overcame what appeared to be his non-physical attributes in no uncertain manner. Big names never bothered him. His approach to football was always right – as time proved as he reached the first team and became an England player. He also showed tremendous spirit and guts after breaking a leg. He is on his own two feet now, but at his command there is a wealth of experience around to help.

'I have always told Wilf, be patient, little apples have to grow. All

11

Left: Manchester United's new boss, Wilf McGuinness, 31-year-old assistant trainer now appointed Chief Coach.

United announce their new appointment to the Press and photographers. From *left to right:* Secretary Les Olive, director Denzil Haroun, chief coach Wilf McGuinness, manager Sir Matt Busby and chairman Louis Edwards.

12

Above: Nobby Stiles played right to the end of the season with all his tremendous enthusiasm, despite knowing that he faced a cartilage operation during the summer.

Right: Brian Kidd raises Manchester United's hopes in the European Cup semi-final against A.C. Milan at Old Trafford.

things being equal he will make a success of his new post.'

McGuinness is also a man born to be Boss. Right from the days when he was a young schoolboy star, he has been a leader of players.

He captained not only Manchester schoolboys but Lancashire and England as well. The man who first spotted his capacity to take charge was chief scout Armstrong.

'The first thing you noticed about Wilf as a schoolboy was that he was an aggressive little footballer belting his way forward,' says Joe.

'We watched him progress from local area teams right through to England, and nothing summed him up better than when he captained England against Wales at Wembley in 1963.

'England were two goals down, but you could see young McGuinness roll up his sleeves and simply drive his team back into the game and they came out with a creditable 3-3 draw.'

The McGuinness appointment carries the title of Chief Coach which was a surprise in as much as the club had said they were looking for a team manager.

I believe the full managerial position will come in the future. As Sir Matt explained:

'This is a sort of preliminary. All the great names in the game have started this way.

'He has a bit of experience to pick up yet in management and it's a question of starting this way. I think he will have enough to bite on with

Sir Matt Busby in transfer mood, signing Burnley's £117,000 winger Willie Morgan. Will there be more big buys under the new management of Sir Matt as general manager and Wilf McGuinness chief coach?

responsibility for the team without taking on other things which could come later.

'The question of team manager could come probably in a year or so. We hope it will.'

For the time being his brief is that he is responsible for team selection, coaching, training and tactics. Sir Matt as general manager remains responsible for all other matters affecting the club and players as well as continuing as club spokesman.

Wilf arrived at Old Trafford in 1952 from Mount Carmel School, Blackley, and he soon made his mark, with his League début coming in 1955. He also continued his international career, quickly graduating to England's youth team, the Under-23 side and then two full caps before breaking his leg playing for the reserves against Stoke City at Old Trafford on December 12, 1959.

It was a bad break, but though it virtually ended his playing career, it was the signal for just as startling a rise on the management side.

United appointed him assistant trainer with the reserve team and it was not long before the Football Association had him as England's youth team trainer.

In 1968 he was appointed manager for the international youths and he was one of Sir Alf Ramsey's training assistants during the World Cup in 1966.

At the age of 31 he must be the youngest person to be in charge of a First Division side in the country.

His greatest challenge will be directing the players who were once his team-mates . . . players like Bobby Charlton who has been a close friend since they arrived at Old Trafford together 17 years ago.

He could have problems, but he has the personality and confidence to overcome them. I am sure he will also enjoy the full backing of skipper Charlton.

It is an appointment that will call for adjustment from the training staff. But United are a close-knit family club and I am sure the appointment from within has pleased the rest of the staff.

As coach John Aston, who has been at Old Trafford for over 30 years as player and staff man, puts it: 'I could not be more delighted with Wilf's appointment. Since he joined the training staff eight years ago we have worked closely together and developed a good understanding.

'Since Sir Matt Busby took over at the end of the war, this club has always been a well-knit, happy family outfit and Wilf's appointment keeps it that way, rather than bringing in someone from outside.'

The End of an Era

SIR MATT BUSBY kicks off this season as the Old Trafford overlord
. . . general manager, a post specially created for him. His insight,
experience and ability are still there at the helm, but it is nevertheless
the end of an era.

For Sir Matt's success was not founded on administrative brilliance,
but on a special relationship between himself, his staff and the players
he gathered around him. It is mainly for this very reason that he
reached his decision to bring a younger man into that vital job of
working with the players and translate himself into a role 'upstairs'.

In a way also, he has paid the price of his own success, because he
has taken the club to such a pinnacle of eminence that it became too
much for one man to control.

'The demands are such that I was neglecting the all-important thing
– the team,' he says.

'Manchester United are not just a football club any longer but a kind
of institution. So many things need attention that I felt my move to
general manager was a step in the right direction.'

When he announced his switch, he was asked in front of a battery of
cameras and representatives of the nation's Press if his decision had
been influenced by the team's comparatively lowly position in the
League.

He replied: 'I would have made the same decision whatever the
circumstances. We are having a little spell when things are not going
right, but I have no worries,' he said at the time.

'By announcing the decision when I did, it meant that a new arrival

16

would be able to get to know the club ready for the following season.'

Sir Matt referred at the time to what he called today's 'heaven and hell' of winning and losing matches, a responsibility which he feels should now fall more directly on younger shoulders.

It's tough at the top and no one has been higher and longer at the top than Matt Busby.

His phenomenal success in football management followed by that miraculous recovery, emotional and physical, from the horror of Munich, elevated him beyond the ranks of ordinary managers.

His name is a household word, not only in Manchester but all over Europe, wherever, in fact, football is played.

His 23 years at the helm of Old Trafford steered Manchester United to the forefront of football with wealth, honours, and prestige for the club and a personal standing in the game second to none.

In the world of football the peak was undoubtedly May 1968, when United won the European Cup at the fourth attempt, a personal and club ambition on which Busby had set his heart.

We wondered then, having conquered everything that football offered, whether it would be the signal for him to move to a higher pasture. At the time he denied it and said that football was too much a part of his life for him to move from the mainstream.

I am sure that he refused to bow out in the whirl of glory surrounding that European triumph because he recognised that it was vital that Manchester United should move on and quickly prepare for the next hurdle.

That this next hurdle is a tough one was reflected in the team's slump in the League last season; but had Busby quit immediately after the European victory, the position could easily have been much more serious.

He stayed to see them once more take up the challenge and satisfy himself that the 'nursery' was packed with yet more youthful stars.

His decision must be very much tied up with his comment after United's crowning triumph in the European Cup.

'This is just the beginning,' he said, and because he is such a visionary in what he wants for Manchester United, he wants a younger man for the job of working with the players.

It takes a great man to bow out at the top, yet though he has become a legend, Busby has never really believed in it himself.

For despite his personal success he has remained essentially a simple,

18

After the European Cup triumph there was surely only one candidate for Manager of the Year . . . Sir Matt Busby out on the Old Trafford pitch here with his award.

straightforward man. Even though he has perhaps acquired an appreciation for many of the good things of life, such as his £4,000 Jenson GT car, he was still living in the same comparatively modest house in Chorlton-cum-Hardy that marked his entry into management in Manchester.

Honours have been thrust upon him in recent years like the C.B.E., the Freedom of Manchester, and a knighthood. Only last season he lunched with the Queen and the Royal Family.

He enjoys the honour of these tributes, but it is the more simple things that can effect him more deeply. For instance, a few years ago the players bought him a handsome cut-glass vase to mark his 20 seasons as manager of United.

They did it secretly and then sprang the gift on him as a surprise at the end of his team talk just before going to play Spurs. The meeting was in a player's bedroom in their London hotel and after the presenta-

Two men of the year with their trophies. Sir Matt Busby with his Manager of the Year award and George Best, Footballer of the Year. Between them, of course the greatest trophy of all, the European Cup, in a picture specially posed for the thriving Manchester United Fan Club.

tion he had to hurry out of the room and walk to the end of the corridor before he could compose himself in readiness for a photograph of the occasion.

Extremely proud and fond of his own grandchildren, he has a soft spot for youngsters and where others may fear to tread in quest of his autograph, a youthful face will soon melt the stern look he sometimes wears in times of stress before the big occasion.

There was the time he turned his back on the clamour and tension of the European Cup semi-final in Madrid. The game was due to kick off in three-quarters of an hour but Busby, along with right-hand man Jimmy Murphy, walked out of the main stadium to have a smoke and quiet contemplation in front of the small chapel behind the main stand.

But to be successful in the cut-throat world of professional football, he has had to be a hard man at times.

This is how Sir Matt Busby saw Press, Radio and Television representatives when he made his momentous announcement that he was moving 'upstairs' to become general manager of the club.

No doubt about the iron fist in the velvet glove, and players have left Old Trafford who have not been at the end of their careers.

It was Nobby Stiles who said that if you have erred and been summoned to the office . . . he doesn't hand out toffees.

It took courage and a certain ruthlessness to pull apart his successful 1948 Cup-winning team in order to introduce his 'Busby Babes', but he did not hesitate because he knew it was right.

He also did not hesitate to put Denis Law on the transfer list when he felt the Scot was holding the club to ransom over terms. Neither did he hesitate to extend the hand of complete forgiveness when the player climbed down and admitted he had been badly advised.

It's all part of the business when football is your life.

'My trouble is that it is almost impossible to forget football for a minute of my waking life, I have it for breakfast, dinner and supper.

And this is how the Press saw Sir Matt Busby when he revealed his decision to retire as team boss. On the right is an equally worried chairman, Louis Edwards. On the left is director Denzil Haroun.

Driving the car, I'm thinking of it,' he says. 'If I go out socially, everybody wants to talk football. The only time I get a break is on the golf course. I'd like to read, but I don't get the time. But really it's football all the way, other people's football, too. Sometimes I go to another match and they start speculating who I've come to see. But I haven't come to see anybody. I've just come to look and listen and to enjoy a match and know what's going on.'

Now perhaps for the first time in 23 years Sir Matt Busby, who will be 60 in 1970, will have the time to relax and enjoy a little more music, a good book and undoubtedly see more of his grandchildren.

The reorganisation of United's management also means a considerable change for another Old Trafford key man. For Jimmy Murphy has been Sir Matt's right-hand man and close confidant throughout the 23 years. Just one year younger than Sir Matt, United's assistant manager was out of the running for the full post, but you can take it that the old firm partnership of Busby and Murphy will not be broken.

His position at Old Trafford is secure, of course. Sir Matt made this clear when he announced the change in his own job. 'There will always be a high and honoured position here for Jimmy Murphy,' he said.

Certainly the two of them have been the most dynamic duo in soccer management, a blend of opposite personalities that has added up to an unequalled number of decisions that time has proved right.

And as Welshman Murphy says: 'I don't like the limelight, but I have not been a "yes" man. That would have been no use to Matt and we have hammered out many an argument before reaching a decision. At the same time we have never fallen out and this is important,' he added.

Murphy is also fully prepared for the change. 'It was no surprise. Matt and I talked it over for a long time and it had to come. The new team manager will be in a track suit working with the players as we did for so long.

'But it won't change our association. The partnership will carry on and the new man can count on my full backing.

'The years cannot take away knowledge and this is where perhaps I will be able to help most.'

United's assistant boss turned down one of many offers to be a full manager that have come his way over the years only a month before Sir Matt's announcement. The most pressing invitation was after Munich when he proved that however difficult the circumstances he was capable of being a boss in his own right.

He took charge of the remnants after the accident and got United functioning again as a club in the absence of the gravely injured Busby.

One club made him an offer immediately after the crash that he is convinced was a deliberate attempt to sabotage United's recovery.

That the club not only recovered but became front runners again, is a triumph for the partnership as well as for Sir Matt.

Perhaps the changes will mark the end of an era, but at least the old partnership will be there in the background to help and inspire the new man in his efforts to maintain their incredibly high standard set over so many years.

I was Transferred
and Dropped

Willie Morgan was the new boy at Old Trafford last season, one of Sir Matt Busby's rare plunges into the transfer market.

In his Turf Moor days he was tagged Burnley's answer to George Best, sharing with the United star a Beatle type haircut, a snazzy line in dress, and above all a highly individualistic pair of feet.

Yet all has not been smooth going for this high-priced player who was dropped soon after his arrival. Now he has a promise for the future.

EVERYTHING seemed to happen to me very quickly last season and I really know now what they mean by the ups and downs of football.

After years of a comparatively quiet life with Burnley where I tended to be a big fish in a little pool I was suddenly catapulted into the big-time atmosphere of Old Trafford and at a time when I was least prepared for it.

You see I had been at loggerheads with Burnley for some time and they had got fed up with me continually asking for a transfer. The result was that in the end they left me out of their set-up. They didn't give me a game on Saturdays, not even in the reserves, and I had to do a lot of my training on my own.

So when my transfer to Old Trafford came at the end of August, 1968, I was hardly in the best condition. I just wasn't match fit, yet naturally after paying such a big transfer fee, I had to go straight into the United first team.

I know I must have disappointed a great many people. I certainly disappointed myself and I know I didn't look like a Scottish Under-23

24

international who had also won a cap for the full Scotland side and had been getting a few reports with Burnley as a match-winner.

Possibly because I wasn't properly fit I got one or two knocks which seemed to put me further out of my stride. I might also say that the team were not playing too well either, which didn't help. I found the training with United harder than at Burnley which took a bit more edge away, and what with travelling through from Bacup every day I never got on top of the job.

I wasn't particularly surprised when I was dropped after 17 games. Disappointed yes, but not annoyed because I knew inside that 'the boss' was right. He explained he was going to put me in the reserves for a spell to help me find my feet.

I was out for a month and I think it did me good. At least I felt I was playing better towards the end of the season. I can do the training now, feel much fitter and living in a house in Sale near the ground, I am much happier all round.

I am told my fee cost United £117,000. It's a lot of money but I

New boy Willie Morgan trots out into the big-time atmosphere of Old Trafford. Behind him are Frank Kopel, now with Blackburn, and Nobby Stiles.

Over page: Willie Morgan in action for the Reds. Competing here with Paul Madeley of Leeds United.

make this promise now. I'll pay them back before I have finished and I am really looking forward to this season.

It is not that I was unhappy at Burnley, at least until the end when I wanted to get away. For a youngster it is a great place and I can quite understand Tommy Docherty sending his boy there for his apprenticeship. I joined soon after leaving school while I was playing with Fishcross Boys' Club near my home town of Sauchie. As a schoolboy I had played in the final trial for Scotland but didn't make it into the international team.

Several clubs showed interest in me but it was Jimmy Stein, Burnley's chief scout, who invited me to Turf Moor. I was supposed to stay for a fortnight and then go on to have a look at Blackpool. But while I was at Burnley I broke my toe, chipping a bone, and had my foot in plaster.

In the end I stayed for six weeks and they treated me so well that when they asked me to sign I agreed straight away. I had no regrets either. It's the flow of young players that keeps Burnley going and they give a lot of attention to their youth coaching. They spend a lot of time teaching each individual and making you develop.

There is a lot of emphasis on training in skills and they harp on this

28

United beat Rapid Vienna 3–0 in the European Cup and this is Willie Morgan's first goal in the competition.

until you have got certain aspects right. If you are good enough you get your chance early, but at the same time they don't rush you, they just bring you along steadily. It's a tremendous system, just look at the never-ending stream of young players they bring into League football.

They have a wonderful coaching set-up and in Jimmy Adamson they have a great coach. Although there was a bit of a rift between Burnley and me when I left I cannot speak highly enough of what the club in general and Jimmy Adamson in particular did for me.

This season I hope you will see better results for all the opportunities I had. Certainly football has its ups and downs and there were a few other examples at Old Trafford last season.

Take Bobby Charlton for instance. Although this player is one of the most respected players in the game it didn't stop a whispering campaign at one stage that he was perhaps at the end of his long innings with England and due for the chop.

It came into the open after the first leg of our European Cup semi-final with A.C. Milan in Italy. Bobby had a very quiet game. All the national newspaper reporters were at the match and they were all tipping that Sir Alf Ramsey would leave him out of the England team for the British international tournament.

They pointed to the fact that he had not been playing well for United in League games. Well that was probably true, except that he had had only three games after missing nine with injury, his longest spell out of the team for six years.

Fortunately for England – not so lucky for Scotland I might add – Sir Alf left Bobby in his team to see for himself and he emerged one of the most outstanding players in the whole tournament. He was fantastic against Wales and I must say we would rather have had him on our side when Scotland were thrashed 4–1 at Wembley in the final game.

I think the critics had under-estimated what an injury can do to upset a finely balanced player like Bobby Charlton. He also picked up for United after the international matches and there was certainly nothing wrong with the goal he hammered past Cudicini in the return leg with Milan at Old Trafford.

There was another great come-back story at Old Trafford last season as well . . . big Bill Foulkes. Some said he had played his last game for United when he came off second best in a personal duel with Ron Davies of Southampton at Old Trafford. Young Steve James came into the team and is a player of excellent promise and ability.

But Steve found it tough in the First Division and felt he was

Manchester United on parade with the European Cup, the elite trophy they went so close to keeping for another season.

Back row (left to right): Bill Foulkes, John Aston, Jimmy Rimmer, Alex Stepney, Alan Gowling, David Herd.

Middle Row: David Sadler, Tony Dunne, Shay Brennan, Pat Crerand, George Best, Francis Burns, trainer Jack Crompton.

Front row: Jimmy Ryan, Nobby Stiles, Denis Law, manager Sir Matt Busby, Bobby Charlton, Brian Kidd, John Fitzpatrick.

Centre-half Bill Foulkes made a great come-back at the end of last season. Here he tussles with Ron Davies, the Welsh International and Southampton centre-forward.

losing his edge. He said he felt tired in games and had a chat with the boss with the result that he was rested. Bill came back looking fitter than ever and despite his 37 years showed some of us younger ones a thing or two.

Bill of course is a model professional. I had only just started school when he began playing in the first team at Old Trafford in 1952 and he is still going strong, a manager's ideal club man who has looked after himself, a fine example for any youngster to follow.

Injuries upset quite a few players last season. Tony Dunne was especially unlucky. He broke his jaw at West Ham and was all set to return to the team after a couple of outings in friendly games in Ireland when he strained his back in training. We were playing a practice game, with the reserves operating in the style of Milan. Tony turned to chase young Mike Kelly and ricked his back.

We were all very worried about Nobby Stiles as well. Nobby was carried off near the end of the first leg in Milan. His knee had 'locked'. It wasn't the first time he had had that kind of trouble but before it had always come right fairly quickly. This time it wasn't so quick and he was told he would have to have a cartilage operation.

He carried on with the games in Ireland to prove his fitness and then played against Milan with a storming performance. It was no fault of Nobby's that we didn't reach the final. Not that it was anyone's fault of course. We had what we are still convinced was a good goal not allowed.

But that is in the past, and the club, like me, are looking ahead. Everyone is well aware that we face a critical season. We are losing Sir Matt Busby as our team boss, which is almost like going to another club. It's such a great change in the set-up, particularly for the players who have grown up from schoolboy level under his careful eye.

As the new boy perhaps I won't feel it quite so strange because I believe Sir Matt acted very wisely and that it was a move that had to come.

I believe Wilf McGuinness can be a big help to the club and to the players. He is young but he has always had a strong personality and as assistant trainer he already holds the respect of the players.

Jimmy Adamson was also young when he started at Burnley and he was the best thing that ever happened to the club. I cannot see any reason why Wilf should not be equally successful.

Certainly I for one will be backing him all the way as I try to prove that I was worth that frightening transfer fee.

European Cup
Knock-out

I T was sad of course to see the handsome European Cup trophy that had graced the visitors' lounge for 12 months leave Old Trafford. One wonders whether Leeds United, the new champions, will bring the European title back to this country.

It could well be. British football is making a much bigger impact on the rest of the world these days and I believe the Old Trafford breakthrough can do nothing but boost the confidence of those who follow.

Chairman Louis Edwards wagers that the club will be back in Europe within four years. Perhaps he is thinking of the last time United did not have a place in Europe . . . in season 1966–67 when they won the League championship to bounce back the following season for their European Cup triumph!

United of course have no automatic key to success, no monopoly of talent or ambition and it is certainly true that the club face a challenging period as they move from one managerial era to another. Success goes in cycles, and as Sir Matt Busby once remarked, you have got to make your own cycles. It seems to me that Manchester United are as well equipped, if not more so, as any club to make the wheel of fortune turn favourably in their direction again.

They finished eleventh in the League, reached the sixth round of the F.A. Cup, enjoyed a storming run to the semi-finals of the F.A. Youth Cup and fought hard to keep the European Cup before losing 2–1 to A.C. Milan in the semi-finals.

They didn't win anything, but you can hardly call it a season of failure, particularly when you bear in mind the manner of their defeat

35

This is it . . . the brilliant Bobby Charlton goal that beat Fabio Cudicini and gave United the feeling that they could win their European Cup semi-final against A.C. Milan.

by Milan. For this was no poor performance; it was not a question of being outclassed or looking out of place in the semi-finals of football's greatest competition.

United bowed out of Europe in the second leg at Old Trafford with a dazzling display, dignity and unfortunately a chunk of just plain bad luck.

There was BAD LUCK because unlucky 13 minutes from the end United had the ball over the Milan line in a tremendous goalmouth scramble from Pat Crerand's chip.

The players swore it was over, television film suggested it was, and all doubt was removed from my mind when the biggest Manchester City fan among the *Manchester Evening News* photographers, Eric Graham, a few feet from the spot, said: 'Although I sez it as shouldn't, it was a goal.'

A goal then would have given United a 2–0 score and a play-off in Brussels.

Instead they won the match 1–0, but lost 2–1 on aggregate. Their last chance of qualifying for Europe the following season had gone but the Reds could go out with heads held high.

There was DIGNITY in defeat. You saw it as the players lined up at the entrance to the tunnel to applaud their victors off the field. You saw it in a most sportsmanlike performance which even after the controversial goalmouth disappointment didn't waver. Then there was the DAZZLING DISPLAY of a team that gave everything.

No one would think Nobby Stiles was under the shadow of a cartilage operation, and Pat Crerand shook off all his cares to give a wonderful display of creative football, his skill matched only by his capacity for work.

Bobby Charlton had a truly inspired spell when he scored United's goal in the seventieth minute after a brilliant piece of work with George Best. It was incidentally United's hundredth goal in European Cup football.

It was hard for the front forwards of course. Milan have not won themselves a reputation as defensive masters for nothing.

Best was up against a great full-back in Angelo Anquilletti, yet still managed to pull out a few tricks. Willie Morgan similarly showed a lot of enterprise, and Brian Kidd stuck to his task manfully.

Full-back Francis Burns had a fine come-back, his first senior competitive game for four months. Yet like Shay Brennan and Bill Foulkes he had composure and he was skilful.

With two particularly good saves from Jimmy Rimmer the defence did its stuff and kept a clean sheet.

Sir Matt Busby conceded two mistakes. 'We missed chances near goal and we should, perhaps, have driven our centres across instead of putting over high balls which were easy for the tall Milan defenders,' he said.

But the United manager added: 'I was still very proud of the team. They were magnificent. They gave everything and you cannot ask for more.'

Bobby Charlton said: 'It is more disappointing to lose because we played well and deserved a play-off. We could have been a bit sharper near goal but we didn't have much luck – so there you are!'

It was indeed a story of disappointment, but I, for one, will remember this last game in Europe for Sir Matt Busby as he finished as team boss for his post 'upstairs' as general manager.

His players did him proud, even in defeat, which is often the greater test.

What a pity the Stretford End failed so miserably to rise to the occasion. They hurled an astonishing assortment of missiles at goalkeeper Fabio Cudicini and knocked him unconscious.

The hooligan element disgraced themselves, the only black spot on a great night.

The semi-final was lost of course in Milan where the Reds went down 2–0 in the frightening atmosphere of San Siro Stadium with its rockets, smoke bombs and fanatical support. As Pat Crerand said after

This is nearly it . . . Denis Law swears he had the ball six inches over the line from Pat Crerand's chip. But referee Marcel Machin of France wouldn't allow a goal and United were out of the European Cup.

Fabio Cudicini was laid out by a piece of brick thrown from the Stretford End and the European Cup semi-final with A.C. Milan was held up for five minutes. Coach Nereo Rocco is on the field here as the Italian skipper, Rivera, talks to his goalkeeper.

the match: 'Two goals down against any team is bad enough, but against Milan it's like being four down, they are so good at the back.'

At that stage of the Italian Championship Milan had conceded only 11 goals in 26 games. Cudicini, their 6 ft. 3 in. goalkeeper they call 'Il Ragno', or 'the Spider', spun a secure web across his goal and their defence looked impregnable. Full-back Angelo Anquilletti gave George Best a thin time, Karl Schnellinger was beaten at times by Willie Morgan, but always had cover, while Brian Kidd was marked mercilessly by Roberto Rosato.

United's attack did not play particularly well either, although in the first half-hour the team looked quite capable of holding their opponents. They were not extended as they felt their way around cautiously but safely.

Jimmy Rimmer, making his European début, made one or two saves that suggested that United's defence could match even the Italians.

But the thirty-third minute goal by centre-forward Angelo Sormani destroyed them. Then Kurt Hamrin sealed the game with a goal five minutes after the interval when United's defence was split wide open.

Two goals proved too much at Old Trafford. What made the result particularly disappointing was that in the previous round the Reds had polished off Rapid, the Austrian champions, in such a professional, highly skilled manner.

The first leg was at Old Trafford and was won 3–0. The Austrian midfield play was clever in this game, but young Steve James showed great maturity to dominate at centre-half in a defence that completely shut out the opposing forwards near goal.

Up front the Reds really sparkled, with every forward in great form, particularly devastating on the wings, a key factor in the battle to breach the defensive screen that Rapid threw around their goal.

George Best ran brilliantly and scored the first goal at the vital time just before the interval.

The Austrian defence were at sea when Willie Morgan pulled the ball across the goal. Law was challenging and as a defender desperately hit the ball against his own post Best shot the rebound home.

Morgan was always a threat on the flanks and he was on hand to mark his European début with a goal after Bobby Charlton and Brian Kidd had sliced through.

Stiles was also in celebration mood after the addition to his family earlier in the day. He chipped a delightful pass over the Rapid defence for Best to score United's third goal with typical cheek as he pulled the

40

Denis Law and Milan substitute Santim are in appealing mood in this shot from the European Cup semi-final at Old Trafford.

ball across goal to make sure.

It was a good win and the second leg in Vienna raised United's hopes higher than ever with another extremely competent performance. This match was a masterly exhibition of how best to conserve a three-goal lead from a first leg and at the same time spell even more scoring danger to the opposition in the away leg.

It was an ability that rocked Rudolf Vytacil, boss of Rapid and, as a former chief of national teams, Czechoslovakia and Bulgaria, one of the most experienced managers in the business.

He told me: 'I was astounded at Manchester United's ability to attack away from home. I expected it at Old Trafford, but to come to Europe and go on attacking as well as defend very tightly is amazing.'

'United have a very good tactical approach and they are the tops of

41

George Best scoring in United's 3–0 win against Rapid Vienna in the European quarter-final.

all Europe.

'It is not a question of United being just better than Real Madrid, the team we beat in the last round, United are very much better.

'Their strength lies in their brilliant individuals, but they are also a good team.'

Jimmy Murphy, United's assistant manager, was also impressed by the team's performance. He summed it up: 'I thought they were extremely professional. They defended in depth and they attacked in strength.'

So United exploded the fallacy once again that they are a luxury team of individuals with little tactical appreciation as they moved into the semi-finals of the European Cup for the fifth time of the five occasions they have competed . . . a tremendous record of consistency and high achievement.

Stepping into Europe Again

UNITED opened the defence of their European crown in a pleasant and easy canter, beating Waterford, the League of Ireland team, 10–2 on aggregate.

Seven of those goals were scored by Denis Law, romping back in no uncertain manner after his cartilage operation during the summer. He hit all three goals in the 3–1 win at Lansdowne Road, Dublin, and four in the 7–1 second leg at Old Trafford.

Two goals against Anderlecht in the next round brought Law's total in the European Cup to 14 and gave him yet another Old Trafford cup record. The previous best was 13 scored by Dennis Viollet. The Scot's seasonal tally of nine also had him chasing Altafini's European Cup record of 14 goals scored in the 1962–63 season.

Yet these European Cup ties also put Denis Law on the spot, in more ways than one! For the flying Scot missed two penalties, one against Waterford in Dublin and one at home to Anderlecht. It meant that Denis had missed four out of six penalty chances in just over a year, not the kind of marksmanship one usually associates with the Law man.

Yet even with this penalty extravagance, Law set Lansdowne Road alight as the Reds set off once again down the European trail. Sir Matt certainly flew home from Dublin a happy man – not just because of the 'safe' two-goal lead, but more because of the manner in which it was gained.

Even allowing for League of Ireland standards, there was a competent, efficient style about the way the Reds wrapped up the opposition.

The United manager openly admitted before the game that he was

worried that the team were starting to defend their European crown
still searching for their rhythm.

Particularly encouraging of course, was the way Denis Law found
his scoring touch. The Scot told me before the match that he was anxious
to make up for the lost time after sitting out so many European Cup
ties, dogged with injury.

But I hadn't realised he was in so much of a hurry. His three goals
were all sharply taken and what a fantastic, deadly duo he struck
with George Best.

The Irishman laid on two of the goals – Brian Kidd the other – and
he led Waterford a merry old dance.

It was little wonder that the fans gave Best the screaming, pop-idol
treatment. In the short distance from coach to hotel after the match
the United players had to battle their way through hundreds of youngsters whose sole object seemed to be to try and grab a piece of him.

His sweater was ripped as he ran the gauntlet, and certainly Best is
one Northern Irishman whom the Republic would be delighted to
call their own.

But while Best and Law stole the scoring limelight, there was also an
extremely confident performance by the rest of the team against a side
which, though lacking top-class ability, nevertheless put up a spirited
performance.

United went boldly for a win despite playing away from home, and
despite their indifferent form in the League around that time.

44

Denis Law, with a hat-trick against Waterford in Ireland, heads United further
along the goal trail in the European Cup return leg against the Irish part-timers.

Sir Matt banked on the atmosphere of the big-time to bring out the best in his established players and shrewdly chose this match to restore wing-half Pat Crerand after leaving him out for a spell.

Crerand helped considerably to get the forwards moving smoothly.

It was also smooth going in the second leg at Old Trafford as the Reds sailed to a 7–1 win and applauded Waterford off the pitch at the close.

Of course it is easy to be magnaminous in victory, particularly if you have just given your opponents a real beating.

But United's gesture went much deeper . . . it was a vote of thanks for a game of football with faith in the British concept of how it should be played fully restored.

After the chilling, cold-blooded approach of Estudiantes in Buenos Aires for the world club title the previous week, the League of Ireland men were like a breath of fresh air. They tore into the game – particularly in the first half-hour, when they had Alex Stepney at full stretch two or three times – with a zest that never flagged, even when the score mounted up against them.

They were always in full control of their tackling and not once did they attempt to clog a surprise win or pull an opponent down.

In fact, there was only one trainer on the field, and just once at that, to treat a Waterford player who was down with cramp.

United, of course, were only up against a team of part-timers, but the Reds had faced lowly teams before and failed to master them in any-

This goal at Old Trafford gave Denis Law a personal total of seven in the two legs against League of Ireland Waterford, in the European Cup.

thing like such a decisive way.

Denis Law's ability to snap up goals was amply demonstrated with four goals to his name. Incidentally, is there another player who has scored a hat-trick in both legs of a European round?

I would doubt it.

United's other scorers were Nobby Stiles, Bobby Charlton and Francis Burns.

But some of the loudest cheers of the night were reserved for winger Al Casey's goal for Waterford. It was the crowd's salute to a plucky team who never stopped playing football in the right spirit.

United also found themselves in fine form for the first leg of the next round against Anderlecht at Old Trafford. The Reds won 3–0, but only after an indifferent first half when they looked very much a team lacking two star forwards in George Best, suspended as a result of his Estudiantes sending-off, and Willie Morgan, not yet eligible for the European Cup.

There was also the worry of whether Law's injured knee would stand up to a 90-minute strain.

Law himself looked loath to test it over much, and though Crerand and Charlton worked hard to get the team moving, the play was too square and too static.

And all through this stage United looked mighty vulnerable to the breakaway bounce of the Belgian champions. Indeed, it was only the out-stretched foot of Stepney as he dived the wrong way that robbed

United get off the scoring mark in their European tie against Anderlecht at Old Trafford.

47

Bobby Charlton (*left*) and Carlo Sartori leap with delight as the Reds pile up a three-goal lead against Anderlecht in the first leg.

Devrindt, a dashing centre-forward, as the Reds stretched themselves in attack.

United's apprehension was aptly reflected when Law topped his penalty shot for Trappeniers to save.

The promoted wingers, Jimmy Ryan and Carlo Sartori, were understandably reluctant in this atmosphere to take on the full-backs . . . yet it was the two new men who helped turn the game so dramatically in the second half.

Suddenly the Reds began to capture the adventurous spirit that has marked many of their European Cup ties and it was Ryan, splendidly rounding his man on the right flank, who centred for Brian Kidd to head home the first goal.

Then Law got cracking, neatly heading home Charlton's deep centre from the left, and a few minutes later again being in the right spot at the right time to sweep home a rebound after fierce shots from Kidd and Sartori.

Sartori finished the game on a particularly high note. There has never been any doubt about his ability, but in this match, his debut in the European Cup, he showed the all important temperament.

The Reds finished well on top with the Belgians out of steam.

There was also displayed a splendid sporting spirit from both teams to show once again that for every bad-tempered match there are many more in which the challenge of Europe only serves to show the game in new dimensions of skill and entertainment.

Although United went to Belgium for the second leg with a three-goal lead, their European crown wobbled as they lost the match 3–1, and scraped through to the quarter-finals with a 4–3 aggregate result.

As Bobby Charlton described it . . . he could see the ghosts of Sporting Lisbon flitting about Astrid Park!

The United skipper could see the possibility of Anderlecht over-hauling what seemed at one stage an impregnable four-goal lead, just as five seasons ago in Europe, Sporting had blasted a three-goal lead out of sight with a 5–0 victory to knock the Reds out of the European Cup Winners Cup.

'As Anderlecht kept scoring I could see those Sporting Lisbon players on the field again,' said Charlton. 'They kept coming back to me as I ran around.'

Charlton's nightmare failed to become reality, but it was too close for comfort!

Perhaps Carlo Sartori's seventh-minute goal on top of the first leg

lead lulled United into a false sense of security, or as Charlton put it:
'I think we tended to sit back and think no one could score four.

'It turned out they very nearly did and we almost paid for missing
some easy chances early on that could really have sewn up the game.'

Certainly United started in storming style. In the early stages one
expected Anderlecht to set the pace while United cautiously felt their
way.

It was quite the reverse. For all the defensive loaded line-up with
two wing-halves, Nobby Stiles and John Fitzpatrick, in the forward
line, United took the game to their opponents and had them reeling.

They made a mockery of Anderlecht's offside trap, repeatedly
catching them square with well-timed through passes from Bobby
Charlton and Pat Crerand. Charlton at this stage was the supreme
midfield master, spraying passes about.

Even after centre-forward Mulder had equalised in the 18th minute
with a surprise shot from outside the box, United looked quite safe
and the score still stood at 1–1 at half-time.

But it was an anxious last 20 minutes as Anderlecht scored twice to

49

Trappeniers, the Anderlecht goalkeeper, was not easily beaten, as he shows
with this full-strength dive. United lost the second leg 3–1 to take the tie 4–3
on aggregate.

make it 3–1 for the Belgians.

Sartori's goal, his first in senior football, was a life-saver. For if the game had finished level on aggregate, his 'away' goal would have counted double.

The Reds certainly gave their 300 or so fans who had made the journey a touch of the jitters in those closing stages.

Norberto Hoefling, the Anderlecht manager, told me after the game: 'The Madonna was with Manchester United.'

But this hardly takes into account the depleted state of United's team and the injuries that forced Sir Matt to field such an unusually defensive side. As the United manager admitted afterwards, this tie was the biggest gamble in all his European experience.

'I've never been so worried before a European tie,' he said.

'Tony Dunne wasn't too bright in training the night before the match with an ankle injury. Bill Foulkes had had only one game in five weeks, and David Sadler had had a dreadful spell with illness, losing over half a stone in weight.

'We already had a lot of young players in the team and we had to gamble a little bit.

'You will meet few better forward lines than that of Anderlecht. Puis is one of the best left-wingers I have seen for a long time.

'There was always the fear that if they had scored an early goal we would have gone to pieces.

'I don't like to gamble in football, but this was a situation in which I was forced to do so – and take risks.'

But the Brussels gamble paid off, and United were through to the last eight of the European Cup and a tie with Rapid of Vienna, conquerors of mighty Real Madrid.

We Are Not a Team of Fighters

by

PAT CRERAND

Pat Crerand is one of the players of great stature and influence at Old Trafford. A strong personality, he has filled the gap left by the departure of Noel Cantwell and is the unofficial spokesman of the dressing room, a protector of players' interests.

He is also a passionate follower of football, and such a protector of what is best in the game, that at times he has got himself into trouble!

ONE of the penalties of success is that people are only too ready to look for flaws and find fault. Most of the time this is something Manchester United can shrug off as an occupational hazard, but occasionally the sniping can reach hysterical proportions.

For instance most of the fans have come to know and accept Nobby Stiles. They are used to him waving his arms about, and even on away grounds, they have a laugh or a boo and that's it. The reason of course is that they know he is not a vicious player. He'll perhaps give away a few free kicks if danger threatens, but you don't see him going around deliberately kicking people.

On the Continent, though, it is different, they just don't seem to understand him and since the World Cup he has had a terrible time in Europe. Nobby, with that toothless, grinning jig round Wembley, after England had won the World Cup, became a household hero in this country. But in Europe it seemed only to spark a vicious smear campaign. He was booed and whistled at every time he set foot on a foreign field, even before he had touched the ball.

He was disgracefully treated by the Italian fans when he played for England in Rome in the Nations Cup and it was the same playing with us.

51

Over page Nobby Stiles, finger pointing, explains tactics to Alex Stepney!
Most of the fans just have a laugh or a boo at Nobby, says Pat Crerand.

The Belgians in 'Brussels booed him before the game had even begun when they were announcing the teams for the European Cup tie against Anderlecht and the Argentinians clearly had him cast as the villain of the match when we played Estudiantes. As the Boss says, the South American Press and Radio had crucified him before we had even got to Buenos Aires. It wasn't so surprising in that atmosphere that the referee got carried away and sent him off.

The people there believed anything about him and the questions they asked him in interviews would make you laugh here.

'Why are you bad man? Do you beat your wife?' These were the kind of things they asked.

The most ridiculous ideas also spread round Europe. They wanted to know in one town if he got his place in the England team because Sir Alf Ramsey was his father-in-law. A little bit fed up, Nobby answered one interviewer that of course it was true. He thought the man was joking, but he took it seriously and Nobby had to hasten to explain.

'They'll believe anything about me over there,' says Nobby, and of course it is not easy to play in this atmosphere. For even if you can shut the crowd out of your own ears there is still the danger that the fans will influence the referee and by their noise make a trivial foul seem a diabolical deed. This is what happened to Nobby in South

If it comes to a fight, we are lost, says Pat Crerand.

America of course when he was sent off for just waving his arm at the referee's offside decision against him.

Nobby is a great team man. I think he had more to do with England winning the World Cup than anyone else.

Before he arrived on the scene, England were a good enough side at times, especially if things were going well for them. But they never impressed as a side who would put up much of a fight.

Then, against Scotland at Wembley in 1965, we saw the difference. Down to nine men, England held on and fought to a 2–2 draw.

Nobby? He worked like a navvy. You could almost see the rest of the England team saying to each other: 'Well, if this wee man isn't giving up, we're not either.' I'm sure Alf Ramsey realised that day just how much Nobby meant to the team.

Now they say Nobby is a dirty player. If you believed all the things that had been written and said, you'd think Nobby was the dirtiest player who'd ever kicked a football.

It makes me sick. My definition of a dirty player is someone who goes out deliberately to hurt an opponent. I'm thinking of those who go 'over the ball' so that when you go to kick it your shin meets their boot.

It's partly Nobby's fault, too, of course, because on the field he seems such an aggressive, cheeky character. Off it he's the quietest soul you could meet.

But certainly we are not a dirty side, nor a team of fighters. In fact if a match kicks up rough and dirty we haven't a chance. We just haven't the players who can reply and play this way, we might just as well pack up and go home. Yet people still knock us at times, even our own supporters.

For instance at the last annual meeting, one of the shareholders criticised us and said we had one or two players who should improve their manners and stop arguing with referees and that kind of thing.

The Boss immediately pointed out the difficulties facing us, particularly in big games such as the Estudiantes match. He said: 'There is only so much that players can stand, this is something that happens where there is success, and where players can be intimidated because of it.

'I continually lay down to the players that if they lose their heads, they lose the match. But against Estudiantes in South America, they were asked to stand too much. I nearly lost my own head which I feel is saying something.

'It is silly in some respects, but human nature comes into it, and sometimes players are subjected to too much.

'People have different temperaments and everyone cannot be the same.'

Indeed no, and I think the Boss was right to emphasise that nearly all the trouble involving United players stems from retaliation. You may think I am a fine one to talk because if you study my crime sheet you'll find I am a bit of an old lag – sent off five times in my career which is certainly nothing to boast about.

But you see all my sins have been retaliation. Three punch-ups with Continentals, one with a Burnley winger and an argument with a referee comprise my crime-sheet.

That little lot sounds terrible, but anyone studying the facts will realise that I'm not a dirty player but a retaliator. Like many Scots, easily provoked.

My first sending-off in Britain was in a five-a-side game at Falkirk. These games, popular during the summer in Scotland, have a special rule which a Falkirk player broke by throwing the ball back instead of forward at a throw-in.

I expected the referee to give us a foul. Instead, he let play go on and I shouted at him about the foul. When he paid no attention, I kept telling him there had been a foul. So he sent me off.

If I had sworn at him I would have deserved it, but all I did, in reasonable language, was to ask him to enforce the rules. I think he treated me harshly.

A few weeks earlier I had been ordered off at Bratislavia in a World Cup tie against Czechoslavakia.

Both sides were keyed up and when I clashed with Kvasnak in a hard tackle, he lost his temper and punched me. I hit him back and the referee sent us both off. I paid dearly for that angry moment because the Scottish Football Association suspended me for seven days and Glasgow Celtic chairman Bob Kelly decided that I had brought the club into disrepute.

So he suspended me, too, and kept me on half wages for a month. But please note that all this happened because I hit a man who hit me first.

Burnley winger Ian Towers provoked me by shirt-tugging as I tried to move away with the ball. I swung my arm round to push him away and unfortunately my hand caught him in the face. Nobby Stiles said that from a distance it looked a peach of a punch, and as I was

57

sent off, this is how it must have looked to the referee. Yet there was no deliberate blow.

I confess though to throwing punches in matches against Ferencvaros of Hungary and Partizan of Yugoslavia, although in each case I was only hitting players who had already punched me.

So in four of the five times I have been ordered off, I didn't start the trouble. Perhaps I was too easily roused but I honestly don't go looking for trouble, and neither does the rest of the Manchester United team.

Although Sir Matt Busby defended us at that shareholders' meeting when we came under fire, don't run away with the idea that he doesn't take steps to try and make us improve our behaviour. I have heard it said that Busby is a great manager except that he is too soft with his players.

Don't you believe it! Do you really imagine United could have achieved all their success without discipline? Every great manager has to be a disciplinarian and Busby is no exception. I'll tell you something . . . he is the hardest man in football!

If you let him down, or misbehave in any way, he'll take you aside and frighten the life out of you. If he thinks the team needs a dressing down then he can let fly in a way that nobody present will ever forget. This is a side of Matt Busby you don't hear much about because you never read about the Busby blow-ups in the papers because he simply does not operate that way. What happens inside Old Trafford stays inside and the players respect him all the more for dealing privately with players who step out of line.

You may read about players from other clubs being fined, suspended or sent home from training camps, and you think what tough managers they must have, what great disciplinarians.

Tough they may be, but they must be also very talkative or like conducting private club business in public. Our Boss believes that punishment is a private affair between himself and the player involved.

So if Manchester United got their biggest dressing down in months, you won't see it in the sports columns.

And if a United first-team star is disciplined, you won't read about that either. Indeed, the other players might even not know. How does the Boss hand out punishment? Well, it usually begins with a beckoning finger, meaning he wants to see you alone. Here, again, he treats you like an adult, never embarrassing a player with a public ticking off. It's always a man to man affair.

If a player has really stepped out of line then he is hit where it hurts most . . . in the pocket! Some of the biggest names at Old Trafford have gone home with an crrand boy's wages because the Boss has slapped a heavy fine on them.

I can't tell you those stories, of course, because these things are discussed only inside the club.

You won't find me complaining about discipline, even when I am on the receiving end, because I have been used to it all my life. In fact it possibly saved me from prison when I was a boy growing up in the Gorbals of Glasgow.

The Gorbals is not a pleasant place. The streets were made for

59

Off duty, on the golf course at Blackpool, *left to right*, Bobby Charlton, Pat Crerand and Nobby Stiles.

crime. There were lots of temptations. I think I only fully realised this years later when I was playing for Celtic and I was invited along with Jim Baxter, who was then with Rangers, to a quiz show at Barlinnie Prison in Glasgow.

There was something familiar about some of the convicts who were sitting there asking Jim and me questions.

After a while it dawned on me – I knew most of them by their first names. They were my old pals!

Either they had gone to school with me or lived nearby. That is when I realised how lucky I was. The only difference between them and me was that I had a mother who packed me off to bed at 6.30 every evening until I was nine, and didn't allow me out after 9.30 until I was 17.

That sort of discipline kept me off the streets, out of mischief . . . and maybe out of prison.

Hard-going in Cup and League

THE European Cup carried the season's last hopes of honours for United. The League and F.A. Cup had already ended in disappointment and in the League especially it was a long, hard haul with the title soon out of reach.

Undoubtedly the Estudiantes fixtures weighed heavily on the minds of the players. The build-up and pressures of the two matches with the Argentinians for the World title were tremendous and it was a decisive factor, I am sure, in the Reds' slow start.

There was also the aftermath of winning the European Cup of course. Having scaled the peak of football ambitions it must always be difficult to start slogging through the foothills again, at least with any degree of conviction.

Injuries also struck hard and early. In only the third match of the season for instance, John Aston broke his leg playing against Manchester City at Maine Road. This was a particularly cruel blow after finishing the previous season on such a high note with his brilliant display in the final of the European Cup. The player was all set to reap the rewards that could well have blossomed with the confidence of his personal success in that match.

His broken leg put him out of senior action for seven months. He returned to the first team against Everton at Goodison Park in March and enjoyed a run in the side in place of Bobby Charlton who had a rare prolonged absence with injury. Charlton in fact missed nine League games with strained knee ligaments, his longest spell out of the team for six years.

Charlton now needs just two more appearances this season to chalk up his 450th League game in his 13 seasons of first-team football. With 58 Cup-ties in this period along with European competitions and England international calls now nearing the hundred mark, Charlton must be one of the hardest worked players in the game.

But undoubtedly the unluckiest United man was Francis Burns who last season had two separate cartilage operations to make it three in just over 18 months. He lost his first cartilage in June 1967 and was struck down again in October 1968, less than a dozen matches after regaining his senior place. He was back two months later but played only seven games before he made it his cartilage hat-trick and he had to wait until the friendly against Shamrock Rovers last May to play in the first team again.

United's other left-back, Tony Dunne, was also out with injury and at a particularly vital stage of the season. Tony broke his jaw in two places at West Ham in March and missed the important European Cup semi-final games against AC Milan. He also made his come-back in Dublin against Shamrock Rovers.

Come and get it then . . . invites George Best in this game against Sheffield Wednesday.

Around this time Shay Brennan had been out with a pulled thigh muscle which meant that United had been playing with two wing-halves, Nobby Stiles and John Fitzpatrick, at full-back.

Fitzpatrick in fact had quite a long run at right-back and for the first time in his career did not have to look over his shoulder at the team sheet every week quite so nervously. It undoubtedly helped the quality of his play after such a long time as a reserve.

It was the early injury to Aston that prompted United into one of their rare plunges into the transfer market with a £117,000 bid for Burnley winger Willie Morgan. The Scottish under-23 cap was slow to settle, but after a spell in the reserves came back much more strongly in the second half of the season.

But Morgan was not the only established player to be dropped last season. Goalkeeper Alex Stepney twice lost his place to Jimmy Rimmer as Sir Matt tried to find a consistently successful side. Pat Crerand also tasted reserve team football in the opening weeks and when he got back into the senior side he found so many promoted youngsters that he

John Aston broke his leg in only the third game of last season, but was playing in the first team again in March and tops this leaping group against Burnley.

Above: Steve James, England youth international, had a long run as first-team centre-half.

Right: United were hard hit by injuries. Tony Dunne, heading clear here, broke his jaw in two places and missed both European Cup games with A.C. Milan.

remarked as he climbed aboard the club coach that he thought he had got out of the reserves.

The team made their almost customary poor start, losing four of their first nine games. The biggest shock at this stage was the 4-0 game against Chelsea at Old Trafford, the heaviest home defeat for six years. Not since Burnley won 5-2 in Manchester in 1962 had the Reds conceded four goals at home.

Ironically it was the day of Morgan's signing, but it was the defence that looked in need of a helping hand. United also lost at home to Southampton and Manchester City but it was away where the team really wobbled. In fact they won only twice away from home – at relegated Queen's Park Rangers and at Nottingham Forest.

At one stage of the season in March, the team were sixth from the bottom of the table and beginning to thank their lucky stars for Q.P.R. who were well planted in the basement. However they pulled themselves together in a seven-match run in March and April, picking up 12 points from 14 to hoist themselves into the respectability of the top half of the table.

For a while the F.A. Cup promised salvation. Although Exeter gave them a fright in the opening stages, the Reds finished comfortably enough with a 3-1 win. Watford forced a 1-1 draw at Old Trafford in the fourth round but lost the replay 2-0.

Birmingham City held the Reds 2-2 at St. Andrew's but were devastated 6-2 at Old Trafford to suggest that United were anxious and able to compensate for their League lapses. Denis Law scored a hat-trick in the Birmingham replay to look bang in Cup form with seven goals from five games.

But then came a tough sixth round, Everton at Goodison Park, and United were beaten by a rather scrappy goal from Joe Royle.

It was left to the youngsters to carry the Cup flag further forward and a particularly young side put the club through to the semi-finals of the F.A. Youth Cup.

The training staff had not expected so much from their youngsters, but they set a hot pace, beating Blackpool 7-2 at Old Trafford after a goalless draw away, and then winning 4-1 at Bury.

Blackburn were beaten 4-1 in Manchester. Then came their best result, a 3-1 win in extra time at Goodison Park after drawing with Everton at Old Trafford with no score.

Centre-forward Jimmy Hall was the top scorer in the competition with half a dozen goals, while the promising inside-forward O'Sullivan

66

Above, right: It's a Chelsea sandwich for Bobby Charlton and a shock for United who were beaten 4–0, their heaviest home defeat for six years.

Right: Alex Stepney saves from Joe Royle, but the Everton centre forward scored a little later to give the Reds an F.A. Cup sixth round knock-out.

and outside-right Bernard Daniels each scored five. West Bromwich who had three players of League experience proved too strong in the semi-final, winning 3-2 at the Hawthorns and 2-1 at Old Trafford.

But nine of United's 12-strong squad are eligible for the competition this season and United's staff were more delighted than disappointed with the overall achievement of their youngsters.

Indeed there was a great deal to make it an exciting season, as was again demonstrated by the fantastic support the club received. United cracked the 1M spectator barrier. This was the third successive season that their League games attracted over 1M fans and once again they were the only club to do so.

The Reds pulled in a League average of 51,000, compared with 36,000 who watched Leeds United win the League championship. United were also ahead of Liverpool who averaged 47,000 from a total attendance which fell a few thousand below the million mark.

It was an all-time record for the Anfield club, but nevertheless it was short of the magical million achieved by Manchester United in a season of League football which by Old Trafford standards was not a good one, yet the message was still clear . . . win or lose, they are still pretty good to watch.

The saddest memory of the season is undoubtedly the death of Ted Dalton, physiotherapist with United for 33 years.

He was present at all the club's big occasions in post-war football after service in the R.A.F., playing a particularly important role in the recovery of players after Munich. He was by the side of Sir Matt Busby when the United boss limped in to Wembley Stadium for the 1958 F.A. Cup Final three months after the accident.

He was known to generations of footballers as not only a man with skilled, healing hands, but a friend always at hand with good advice. Most of the big names in cricket also went through his hands as physiotherapist to Lancashire County Cricket Club and he had a busy private practice covering St. Joseph's Hospital and many television and stage stars.

Last year the pace of his life seemed to catch up with him and he found it difficult to take things easier even after his first heart attack. His death was a big loss to the club, and to many other people in sport.

68

Europe's Footballer
of the Year

MANCHESTER UNITED'S success in winning the European Cup focused the eyes of the European Press on the Old Trafford players and brought the club further recognition. George Best is the latest European Footballer of the Year and his election completed a unique Continental hat-trick for the club.

For Best is the third United player to win the coveted 'Le Ballon d'Or', following in the famous footsteps of Denis Law in 1964 and Bobby Charlton in 1966.

And at the same time the Reds scored a double in the award. For team-mate Bobby Charlton was voted into second place, the first time two players from the same club have snaffled the top two places.

Soccer writers from 25 countries vote for 'The Golden Ball' awards organised by the magazine 'France Football'.

They gave Best 61 votes, Charlton 53, and Dragan Dzajic, the Yugoslav left-winger from Belgrade, 46.

The trophy completed a personal double for Best, who earlier in the year had been elected Footballer of the Year by the English Football Writers' Association. Charlton also took both trophies during his great season in 1966, and finishing in second place to Best meant he had been runner-up for the second successive season after winning it – a proud record in itself.

United are the first club to have three different players winning the award, though two wins by Di Stefano and one by Ramon Kopa has taken the trophy to Real Madrid three times.

Best now joins the elite ranks of foreign players like Di Stefano, Suarez, Sivori, Yashin and Eusebio. Sir Stanley Matthews is the only English player outside United to figure in the winners' list which starts with him in 1956.

70

George Best, European Footballer of the Year, has Liverpool goalkeeper Tommy Lawrence magnificently at full stretch in their League game at Old Trafford.

72

Bobby Charlton, puffing along here, completed a club double by finishing second in the European voting.

Florian Albert of Hungary was the previous year's winner. Other English players ranked after Best were Jimmy Greaves of Spurs 10th, Jack Charlton of Leeds United and Bobby Moore of West Ham joint 22nd and Alan Ball 24th.

Incidentally, Best won his award without any biased patriotic support from England's representative. Brian Glanville of the *Sunday Times* who was on the panel of 25 countries nominated Red Star's Drajic who finished in third place.

Best is the youngest player ever to capture national and European awards, a fair indication of the astonishing strides he is making towards complete football maturity.

In common with the rest of the team last season he lost a little of his sparkle on the return to the bread and butter of League football after the heady success of winning the European Cup, but it was not long gone. He had a fabulous week for instance in February when United played three Cup ties in six days and he was in breath-taking, twinkle-toed form against Birmingham City and Everton in the F.A. Cup along with the European Cup tie against Rapid Vienna.

73

Denis Law leans over backwards, the first of the three United players to be voted European Footballer of the Year, Frank Kopel is back to camera.

Is he already the complete footballer? Team-mate Pat Crerand, now one of Old Trafford's elder statesmen, put it like this: 'If he is not yet the complete player, he is not far off. His only weakness is perhaps hanging on to the ball too long, but often when you think this is what he has done, he gets himself out of trouble and scores a goal. So who is to say he should have passed. When he loses the ball in that kind of situation he annoys us of course. You glower at him and he knows because he won't look at you!

'He also gets annoyed with referees sometimes but you can forgive this when you consider the punishment he takes in a game.'

But though George Best invariably finishes a match with a stack of bumps and bruises he seems to escape the serious injury that often seems to be inevitable for one with such a frail-looking frame.

As Crerand says: 'I have hardly ever seen him on the treatment table. He recovers quickly from injuries and he also has a happy knack of riding tackles. In fact he reminds me of a rubber ball, he just seems to bounce off opponents who come in to tackle him.'

Are the players jealous of him?

'Not at all,' says Crerand. 'Footballers admire skill more than any-one else. Team-mates and opponents alike may envy him at times but we could never begrudge him his success because he has earned it with

74

They don't call George Best a ball juggler for nothing, and sometimes the quickness of the hand can deceive the referee. But it didn't this time, much to the relief of Chelsea's Ron Harris in hot pursuit.

75

It's what you call turning a deaf ear as referee K. H. Burns of Dudley firmly gives his decision, despite what one may surmise to be a certain disagreement from George Best in this Old Trafford League game against Arsenal.

an ability that makes him outstanding.'

United's Irish star has of course won admiration off the field as well as on it. He receives for instance around 500 letters a week, though it has been known to be double, and most of them are from girls.

For six months last season he had a chauffeur driving him around in his distinctive white Jaguar. The chauffeur was not entirely of his own choosing, the indulgence of a wealthy young man, but more the result of a six-month driving ban for a motoring offence.

This was not his first brush with the law, for he already had two or three convictions for speeding which he dismisses rather lightly: 'Let's face it, everyone speeds.'

Best celebrated his return to motoring by graduating to an 'E' type Jaguar. He has also been having a distinctive house built in Bramhall, Cheshire, a talented young man who knows where he is going indeed!

The voting for European Footballer of the Year went like this:

1. George Best (Manchester United)	61	points
2. Bobby Charlton (Manchester United)	53	„
3. Dragan Dzajic (Red Star, Belgrade)	46	„
4. Franz Beckenbauer (Bayern Munich)	36	„
5. Giacinto Facchetti (Inter Milan)	30	„
6. Riva (Cagliari, Italy)	22	„
7. Amancio (Real Madrid)	21	„
8. Eusebio (Benefica)	15	„
9. Rivera (AC Milan)	13	„
10. Greaves (Spurs), Pirri (Real Madrid)	8	„
12. Dunai (Ujpest, Hungary), Schulz (Hambourg SV)	7	„
14. Asparoukohov (Levski, Bulgaria), Chesternev (Torpedo, USSR)	6	„
16. Kindwall (Feyenoord, Holland)	5	„
17. Albert (Ferencvaros), Mazzola (Inter Milan), Scusz (Ferencvaros)	4	„
20. Cruyff (Ajax), Muller (Bayern, Munich)	3	„
22. Charlton (Leeds), Moore (West Ham)	2	„
24. Ball (Everton), Bene (Ujpest), Domenghini (Inter Milan), Fazlagic (Sarajevo), Gemmell (Glasgow Celtic), Johnstone (Glasgow Celtic), Khurtsilva (Dynamo Tbilisi, USSR), Osim (Zel Sarajevo), Pilot (Standard Liege)	1	„

I Earn £20,000 a Year

by

GEORGE BEST

European Footballer of the Year, English Player of the Year, a budding business tycoon, idolised by teenage girls like a pop star, wealthy with an overall income of £20,000 a year . . . this is George Best.

How does it feel at 22 to be feted, ogled and paid so handsomely? I asked George to try and explain.

IT'S quite true I earn about £20,000 a year – give or take a thousand or two either way!

I suppose that sounds rather flippant. Perhaps you think it embarrasses me to find the money pouring in so easily. I say easily because compared with a man who sweats his guts out working in a factory, my earnings are money for old rope.

But there is another way of looking at it. To begin with I consider I am in show business. Football is entertainment and compared with stage stars I am not necessarily overpaid. Why, a top singer can earn that kind of money with just a week's engagements in cabaret.

There may be just a few hundred people watching his show each night, whereas in football, we pull them in at the rate of 60,000 a time! So the money is there – why shouldn't the players have a good slice of it? And compared with the stage or films I reckon footballers have a tougher time. The worst that can happen in cabaret is a bread bun between the eyes; our worst is probably a broken leg which is very much a professional hazard and one that can end a career. Even on a good day there will be bumps and bruises, so why shouldn't we be amply rewarded?

Our life is comparatively a short one. Even if a singer slides out of the best-selling charts, he is probably assured of a living for many more years going round the smaller clubs. In football, on the other hand, even if one is fortunate enough to break into management, you are out of the frying pan into the fire of an even more hazardous career.

The brilliant George Best in a heading duel against Arsenal, earns as much off the field as he does on it.

The elegant George Best, dressed formally as best man for the wedding of Mike Summerbee, his Manchester City pal.

I don't intend even to try management: my plan is that when my playing career is at an end I shall have enough money and sufficient business interests to see me through.

Already I earn more from outside football than I do from the game itself. Some might say this means I am not concentrating as much as I should on my football. I disagree. I have everything in the right perspective. I know full well that if it were not for my popularity as a player the rest wouldn't stand up for a minute. At the same time this is no reason why I shouldn't cash in on my name and make it work for me.

After all, the money I have invested in business is my own. At the start it was a considerable risk but I decided to take the plunge. How did I start on the business side?

Well a lot of it just seemed to happen, but when I realised that my face was becoming well known I thought it out. I met the man who was to become my partner in the first real venture at a party – typically you might say! But Malcolm Mooney and I became friends and we opened a boutique at Sale specialising in mod clothes for with-it youngsters.

I quite liked that type of clothes but I wouldn't have worn some of them if it hadn't suddenly become part of my business life. For instance you should have heard what some of the lads called me when I first arrived at Old Trafford in my sky-blue jacket and then my 'cowboy' outfit.

Now it's different. I don't think they would turn a hair if I dressed in the most outrageous outfit because they expect it of me. I can't shock 'em any more! I don't get embarrassed any more either. It's quite true that when I first arrived I would walk the long way round to the dressing rooms if I thought I might meet someone like Denis Law or Bobby Charlton face to face. They were like gods to me.

But being a Manchester United footballer soon gets you out of this. At times it is like being in a zoo. Nothing would embarrass me now, which is just as well because I have cultivated the publicity when it started to come my way in order to promote my business interests.

At the same time I hope I haven't become a big-head. I don't think I have because I feel this is something in a bloke's character. If he is going to be big-headed, he will be, whether he has got anything to be boastful about or not.

Some folks probably think that the girls who tend to crowd me outside football grounds would be enough to turn my head. But you

The off-duty George Best, wining and dining with girl friend at a United celebration banquet.

82

The casual George Best, stepping back into his car after a six-month motoring ban.

know this business of being popular with the ladies can work two ways. A girl might want to go out with you because you are George Best: on the other hand there are girls who react by saying just because you're the great George Best don't think I'm crazy to go out with you because I'm not! Popularity can work both ways you see. Being well known does occasionally get a bit much. Sometimes I just can't go anywhere and be left to myself. Once two girls followed me around in Manchester for six hours. I nearly went mad, but I don't let this kind of thing go to my head because I know that with youngsters the hero of one week is dead meat a few days later.

Anyway, it's a thing you've got to live with. It's now part of a footballer's life as we become more and more part of the entertainment world. I reckon that in the last five years the number of girls who go to games must have more than trebled.

Mind you, though it may surprise you, I'm still shy with girls. If I think they will turn me down, I chicken out and don't ask them. I suppose the only time I have any real confidence is when I'm out on the pitch. Three years ago I wouldn't have shouted at any of my team-mates and if I was knocked over I would just pick myself up and I wouldn't have said boo to a goose.

Now I find it harder to avoid retaliating if I'm kicked or if I think the referee has given me a bad decision. You may have noticed odd moments of trouble in which I have sometimes been involved! But then it doesn't get any easier when opponents pick you out for tight marking. I know that certain full-backs are going to make a point of giving me a crack if they can manage it, more so nowadays then when I was starting as a youngster.

It tends to spoil the enjoyment of playing football but I accept it in return for the big rewards that come my way. It's another of the reasons why I don't consider myself over-paid!

If I'm lucky I've got at least eight years more football left in me. That will take me up to 30 and by that time I want to have enough money to try a few other business ventures. I shall always be a football fan but I shall do my best to make sure I have something to support me when my playing days are over. The boutique in Sale has now blossomed into a more ambitious shop called Edwardia in the middle of Manchester. I'm a photographic model at the moment for a mail order catalogue and I pick out the clothes I like which will carry my name.

I've enjoyed the money it has helped bring me, I bought a car for my father, his first and he had to learn to drive. I bought my parents a

83

Over page. The argumentative George Best pulled away by peacemaker Nobby Stiles, but in trouble with referee David Smith.

fish and chip business and again it gave me a great deal of satisfaction. I send all my football jerseys and trophies home because I still miss my family in Belfast.

And though I have talked a lot here about money, girls and fame, this is all secondary. My whole life really is football. I would play every day if I could and Saturdays or match days find me just as excited and eager as I was kicking a ball about as a schoolboy. Sundays I hate because it's the day after a match and I have a tremendous feeling of anti-climax after spending a week building myself up for a game.

I can think of no better club to play football with than Manchester United. Matt Busby has been very patient with me at times, and of all the people I know, I admire him the most. I could go to the Boss and tell him anything. He is the sort of man you instinctively trust.

I have had success at a young age but he is one of the people who have made sure it has not gone to my head . . . he and another dozen or so team-mates who would quickly cut me down to size if I ever began to regard myself the way a few of the girls do!

Bitter Battle for
World Title

IF THE national newspaper football writers could have got hold of the
B.B.C.'s David Coleman in South America, he would have been
swinging from a Buenos Aires lamp post!

For it wasn't only Manchester United who came a cropper in the
world club championship against Estudiantes; most of the Press also
saw red, and it was David Coleman who brought their embarrassment
into millions of homes on television.

This is the story of the party-that-never-was, and I can afford to
write it because the five-hour time difference between this country
and the Argentine kept me and the other evening paper journalists
out of trouble.

The problem was the party that Estudiantes threw for United on
the eve of the first leg in Buenos Aires. The Argentinians expressly
extended the invitation to the Manchester players so that both teams
could meet in a happy atmosphere and perhaps create goodwill on both
sides for the forthcoming match.

Sir Matt Busby readily agreed and after training at the Boca ground
the entire United party attended a rather lavish buffet at the Stadium
and were warmly welcomed by the Argentinian directors and various
officials.

The Press were invited, too – but the morning papers had had to
anticipate the event. The party had a 9 p.m. kick-off which meant
that it was two o'clock in the morning in England, which would have
been far too late to start cabling stories for a morning paper.

So the national men wrote and filed their accounts of the party
before it took place, and naturally they had to include graphic des-
criptions of this encounter between the champion players of two conti-

nents. One reporter described how the Estudiantes player who is also a dentist studied Nobby Stiles' dental problem!

Unfortunately the Argentinian players failed to turn up and the British Press spent the evening looking at the door, desperately willing Estudiantes to arrive – however late!

The United manager had given special instructions to his players and their interpreter to mix freely with their opponents. After nearly an hour of small talk, cocktails, fruit juices and delicacies on toast, the Estudiantes officials admitted their players would not be coming.

President Moriano Mangano said that there had been a change of time in their players' last training session which had made it impossible for them to come.

Sir Matt cut short the Estudiantes apologies. 'Don't explain,' he said, and soon after the United party returned in their coach to their hotel 25 miles away at the Hindu Club.

He was angry – but he wasn't as upset as the newspapermen who had

Willie Morgan scores against Estudiantes. It's an equaliser that made the second leg a 1–1 draw, but the Reds were already a goal down from South America.

reported the party-that-never-was and then came home to find that David Coleman had spotlighted their losing gamble on television by reading out their imaginary reports.

I learned later that the failure of the Estudiantes players to attend was basically a rift between them and their directors over the bonus for the match. Coach Osvaldo Zubeldia sided with the players and kept them away; in any case I don't think he really approved. His verdict on cocktail parties for players: 'This is a game for men. I see no point in teams kissing each other!'

Certainly this was when the kissing stopped! Estudiantes were also either incredibly thoughtless or downright provocative with their inclusion in the official programme of a quote by Otto Gloria concerning Nobby Stiles.

In a run-down of the team, the Benfica manager, whose team were beaten by United in the final of the European Cup, described Stiles as 'brutal, badly intentioned, and a bad sportsman'.

Denis Law salutes what we thought was a tie-saving goal from Brian Kidd, but the final whistle had blown seconds before, and Estudiantes had won the world title.

A club programme is the last place for such an inflammatory remark, particularly in the context of the world championship with its history of violence, not least the near-riot of the previous final between Racing and Celtic. Gloria had also described Stiles to the Argentinian Press as an 'assassin' and as soon as the luckless Nobby came on to the field, it was clear the local crowd had him cast as the villain of the piece.

It was almost inevitable that he would be sent off, though his offence was merely the familiar angry wave of his arm at a linesman when he was ruled offside. David Sadler summed up Nobby's ill-luck: 'He turned his back and walked away from everything. He was butted, punched, pushed, kicked – and then sent off for getting offside.'

Sir Matt sympathised: 'They are crucifying Nobby Stiles because of a reputation he has been given which is quite unfair. He was sent off in this match because of a reputation and build-up around him in the Argentine Press which is quite disgraceful.'

This first leg was played in a highly charged atmosphere, with such incongruities as the genteel, gaily coloured folk dancers performing before the kick-off watched by a special platoon of steel-helmeted riot police carrying staves and tear-gas guns.

A bomb belching clouds of red smoke as the players came out on the field seemed like a starting gun for hostilities and the Estudiantes mid-field players wasted no time getting into action.

George Best, Denis Law and Bobby Charlton were singled out for marking which was not so much close as intimidating. Bilardo and Pachame were the principal offenders and they simply made it impossible for United's ball players to function normally.

Sir Matt described it: 'Holding the ball out there put you in danger of your life.'

The result was that United fought mainly a rearguard action, and under the circumstances fought it well. They were beaten only once, Conigliario heading in a Veron corner in the 28th minute. The Manchester players displayed tremendous restraint and they avoided the retaliation that could so easily have created a riot. They accepted quite calmly the referee's decision to disallow David Sadler's 38th minute 'goal' – a perfectly correct decision incidentally with Bill Foulkes offside as television and photographs later showed.

United came home confident they could pull back the one goal deficit, even without the services of Nobby Stiles who was automatically banned from the second leg at Old Trafford as a result of being sent off in Buenos Aires, but the Reds could do no better than

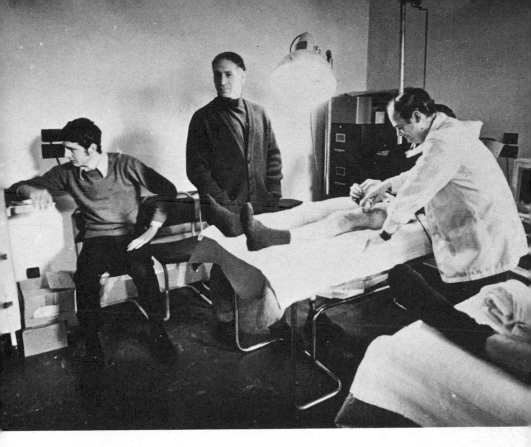

draw their home match.

It was a night of cruel 'animal' taunts from the Stretford End, echoing the controversial epithet first applied to Argentinian football by Sir Alf Ramsey during the World Cup. George Best and Hugo Medina were both sent off near the end, but neither player punched his weight in the flare-up and there were a lot of theatricals.

In fact for once United failed to rise to the occasion. Skipper Bobby Charlton would make no excuses:

'We can't blame them. The game was not anything like as tough as it was in Buenos Aires. They gave us the chance to play and we just didn't take it,' he said.

'They went in for time-wasting and obstruction but they weren't bad. We have no quibbles. We have played teams ten times better and beaten them but we just failed to get going.

'Their early goal killed us,' he added.

It was indeed, a fifth-minute slackness that saw Ramon 'The Witch' Veron fly through a badly marked goalmouth to score the vital goal.

The treatment room at Old Trafford, a busy place after the trip to South America. This more recent picture shows physiotherapist Laurie Mawson at work with Brian Kidd (left) and Bobby Charlton waiting their turn.

Already a goal down from the first leg, it seemed to take the sparkle out of United's attacking. The defence pulled themselves together and they did not give Estudiantes another chance. But the damage had already been done and no one could make any real impression on the strong, commanding Argentinian defence.

Denis Law left the fray just before the interval with a gashed leg that needed stitching, but even though the forward line maintained its momentum, Alberti Poletti, in the Estudiantes goal, was not really tested.

Willie Morgan and Brian Kidd found a way through just before the end with a goal from Morgan that at least made the match a draw. Morgan returned the compliment with a cross that saw Kidd put the ball in the Estudiantes' net just a few minutes later, but it was seconds after the final whistle.

That was the story of United's defeat; they left everything too late. One could feel warmer about the Argentinians' victory if their 1-0 win in South America had been gained less violently.

But even so there can be no grudging their superbly drilled defence at Old Trafford. Perhaps the injury cloud that hung over United as they prepared for this match took the edge off the Reds; whatever the reason they certainly never even looked like winning after that fifth-minute body-blow!

So United lost the Inter-Continental Cup, sadder but wiser, and still, I suspect slightly baffled about their reception in Argentina. For though roughly handled on the field perhaps, the hospitality off it was extensive and friendly. A special polo match was arranged for United's entertainment one afternoon and we went to a barbecue almost every lunch-time! The reception for the Press was equally thoughtful. A bus was put at our disposal for instance complete with mobile bar and a hostess who judging by her attentiveness must have been getting paid on results of liquor consumed.

The paradox of on the field and off it leads one to the conclusion that the Argentinians have a different conception of the game, plus of course their temperament. As one of the rugby-playing public relations men explained to me: 'We are a Latin people. We are passionate in welcoming you and just as passionate about winning once the game has started.'

I understood what he meant when I discovered that this most considerate, warm-hearted fellow was currently serving a suspension imposed by his Rugby Union of TEN YEARS!

93

Left: Nobby Stiles, watched by Shay Brennan with Bill Foulkes on the ground, was sent off against Estudiantes in Buenos Aires. The Press there 'crucified' him, said Sir Matt Busby.

An aerial ballet with Watford. John Fitzpatrick on the left and Bobby Charlton right.

More Starlets
are Launched

LAST SEASON was only two months old when Sir Matt introduced his next crop of 'babes' and showed quite clearly that the precision production line at Old Trafford was still turning out top quality material.

Their team-mates call them 'Big-Head' and 'Harpo', these two latest recruits to senior football.

Steve James rejoices under the name of 'Big Head' for precisely the reason that nothing could be further from the truth. He is so quiet and modest that his friends accuse him of throwing his weight about and bragging. 'Steve told me to pull his golf trolley today,' they'll say, knowing full well that this would be the very last thing on earth he would say.

Carlo Sartori, a name made to measure for European football, gets the name of 'Harpo' after the Marx brother and his tightly curled hair, which in the case of Carlo is a brilliant flame colour and he is complete with freckles.

He was born in the village of Caderzone in Northern Italy, but came to Manchester when he was 10 months old. His father was a knife grinder here, but was killed in a road accident when Carlo was six. He is unmistakably Manchester and Collyhurst, but still travels on an Italian passport, quietly proud of his dual nationality and associations with Italy where he has many relations.

He learned his football at St Malachy's School in Collyhurst and played for Manchester Schools, though he didn't reach England level, probably because he was too small. United also considered him on the wee side, because although they recruited him at the age of 15, it was as an amateur and not as an apprentice professional.

When he was 17 United took him as a full-time professional and he

Two of the new boys, goalkeeper Jimmy Rimmer followed by centre-half Steve James.

began to work his way through the junior teams.

He won a regular place with the reserves in the 1967–68 season, but did not kick off the following season very brightly . . . serving a 14-day suspension.

'I think I have got a bit of the Italian temperament and if I'm among a crowd of players the referee can't help spotting me with my hair,' he says.

His big chance came in October of last year in an injury-depleted attack at Liverpool. George Best, Willie Morgan, and Denis Law all missed this League game on the eve of the second leg against Estudiantes and Sartori played at outside-left.

Jimmy Rimmer (centre) and Steve James (left) are in action here, but John Fitzpatrick is also in the thick of it.

Right: Shay Brennan was in the team at right-back marking England cap Mike O'Grady in this game with Leeds at Old Trafford.

Liverpool won 2–0, but he had done enough to earn being called on as a substitute for Law against the Argentinians. He played the following game at inside-right against Southampton.

It was another defeat, but he had shown up well and played at Sunderland three weeks later in the absence of Law, for whom at that stage he was almost automatic understudy.

His League form earned him his debut in the European Cup, playing both legs against Anderlecht and scoring his first senior goal in Brussels. He played at outside-left in the absence of George Best, who was suspended, and it was in these matches that he really 'arrived'.

After his European debut, his manager said: 'I thought Sartori was a revelation in a match of this nature and importance. He was not playing in his true position, but he took his chance brilliantly and I am very pleased with him.'

Steve James also made his debut in the League game at Liverpool – and could well save United a six-figure fee as the long-term answer to the situation of who follows Bill Foulkes at centre-half.

His appearance at Anfield found him marking Alun Evans, another youngster with whom he played in the Staffordshire Schools side and in the England youth team.

'At least it wasn't so strange playing against someone I knew something about,' said Steve afterwards.

The youngster made five international youth appearances in season 1967–68 but did not become a regular in United's Central League team until the following season and the absence of Paul Edwards for a cartilage operation.

However, time is on the side of Steve James who made his senior bow at the age of 18 and had a long run last season in the centre-half spot.

He has matured rapidly and had the experience of the long-serving Bill Foulkes to help him. 'Steve is going to be a very good centre-half,' says Bill. 'One of the great things is that he wants to learn and he has got better with every match as he picks up positional experience.'

Young James comes from a footballing family – and what's more, his father is still playing! Dad was a full-back with Wolves and Birmingham City and at the age of 47 is playing now for his works' team in the Wolverhampton Sunday League. Last season he steered them to success in both League and Cup while son Steve was busy establishing himself in the position that at one time looked likely to cost Old Trafford £100,000 to fill.

Frank Kopel, although making his League debut in October 1967,

Frank Kopel, in Cup action here against Watford, came to the fore during the full-back injury crisis and was transferred in March to Blackburn Rovers for £25,000.

and playing only once in the first team that season, also made his mark around this time as a serious contender for a top-flight career. His chances had been limited, but injuries to Francis Burns and Shay Brennan gave him a run about the time James and Sartori were in the side and he also 'arrived'. He also attracted the attention of other clubs and in March he was transferred to Blackburn Rovers.

Sir Matt came home from Belgium quite thrilled by the way his young reserves had rallied round during the club's worst injury spell for a long time.

'All the signs look very healthy to me,' he said. 'Because of the pressure on us, some of our young men have been blooded in senior football and have shown what they can do. They have profited from their experience and Manchester United can profit in the long run.'

The United chief had other youngsters in mind as well, one of them Jimmy Rimmer who made his debut just before the end of the 1967–68 season. Rimmer has travelled thousands of miles as reserve goal-keeper in the European Cup but has had very limited opportunity. He ousted Alex Stepney for two games in January and then when he was dropped back into the reserves decided he wanted to seek his future with another club – at least until he got back into the first team!

Alan Gowling, who ended his amateur days last season to become a part-time professional and is still reading for his economics degree, is another player of great potential.

The United boss also had further cause for satisfaction when he looked a little further down the ladder to even younger players who helped the reserve side set the pace at the top of the Central League for most of last season.

Donal Givens from Dublin for instance became the leading reserve marksman at the age of 19, another schoolboy signing equally proficient on the wing and centre-forward.

The reserves had a young side and managed to maintain their momentum despite injury calls from the first team.

It was a period of great development for wing-halves Nick Murphy, son of the club's assistant manager, and Willie Watson.

The manager could certainly see enough to keep him from wild speculations in the transfer market urged in some quarters and his faith in his own club's ability to go on turning out young players of exciting possibility was once again fully justified.

And while all this was taking place, more young Reds were on the march with a thrilling run to the semi-finals of the F.A. Youth Cup.

I Came Up
the Hard Way

by

B R I A N   K I D D

Collyhurst has proved a fruitful hunting ground for Manchester United. Nobby Stiles, Brian Kidd and Carlo Sartori all grew up in this uncompromising neighbourhood to join Old Trafford on leaving school.

It's hardly Manchester's stockbroker belt, but life had character in Collyhurst and provided a spur to play soccer well, as Brian Kidd describes.

THEY say that the best kind of fighter is a hungry fighter, and I believe the same is often true about professional footballers.

I never went hungry, but at the same time, if you have lived in Collyhurst you know what it is to miss out on some of the good things of life and there is a spur to succeed and get out.

The trouble is, not everyone has the chance. As a district we don't produce many doctors or bankers. I mean you could have homework if you asked for it at school, but there weren't many takers, and they didn't force it on you.

But football provided an avenue of escape, not that we realised it at the time. We just got on with playing football at every opportunity and the school encouraged us. There was swimming and cricket as well, but football was the top sport.

There aren't many playing fields in Collyhurst either, but we used to go for matches to a shale pitch about four miles from the school and play in basket-ball boots. The rest of the time we played in the school playground which was divided up into pitches. Not with white lines or anything like that, but just different corners were played on by different gangs of boys.

The older lads played on what was called the big pitch, which was the best and biggest stretch of school yard. I can remember watching Nobby Stiles who was in the same class as my brother at St. Patrick's

105

Brian Kidd, beating Glyn Pardoe here in the derby against Manchester City at Old Trafford, is one of a successful trio of players from Collyhurst.

Nobby Stiles blazed the successful soccer trail from Collyhurst to Old Trafford. He is in action here against Watford in the F.A. Cup fourth round 1–1 draw at Old Trafford.

School, and asking him if I could come on for a game. If you were a smaller lad you had to ask or you might have got a belt round the ear. Nobby hasn't changed. Even as a schoolboy he was always on the go, shouting encouragement and orders at everyone and getting completely carried away with it all.

Carlo Sartori went to another school in Collyhurst, St. Malachy's. He was well known in the district as a good player and I often played against him. I remember we beat them in the schools final one season.

When I was 14 I was playing for Manchester Boys and when clubs started approaching me I began to realise that football could be my big opportunity. Joe Armstrong, United's chief scout, was one of the callers and I came to the conclusion that if ever I was going to make a footballer, Old Trafford was the place.

My father, a bus driver, was really a Manchester City fan and he used to curse United fans when they held up his bus on the old 47 route past Warwick Road. But he agreed that for a young player you could do no better than United.

And nothing has happened to make us change our minds. I have had every help and encouragement from the coaching staff and I got my chance in the first team early.

I think Collyhurst had made me try that little bit harder, made me realise how lucky I have been to be able to play football. I appreciate money, good food and new places all the more.

But don't think I'm ashamed of our district. Most of it has been knocked down as slum clearance anyway now. We live at Moston for instance and our old house has been pulled down. The demolition people just got there before the roofs in our street fell in without any help! Those back to back houses were nothing to boast about.

But the people . . . now that's another matter. There used to be a lot of fights, but there was also a lot of sincerity and friendship. Doors were never locked in Collyhurst because it would never occur to anyone. People would help one another, too, much more neighbourly than I imagine you get sometimes on new estates. They were straightforward folk, nothing false pretending to be something they weren't.

As a lad you could get a mineral at any house and you learned how to treat life. It's a feeling that is born in you and I don't think anyone who grew up in Collyhurst will ever get out of it. I wouldn't want to, and though it was a rough district I liked it.

There was always plenty of cowheel pie in our house. Steak and cowheel was my mother's speciality, that and taty hash. My mother

Brian Kidd leaps to the left, but is beaten to it by John Aston (right) in a goal-mouth scramble against Sunderland.

also taught us manners. They don't cost anything and I shall always
be grateful to her for telling me how to go on as football began to take
me further afield.

Now I play golf, I've been to America, Australia and quite a few
European countries. I'm spreading my wings but I hope I shall always
retain something of the real values I learned in Collyhurst.

I would rather have self-respect than all the money in the world.
Money doesn't bring happiness. I have seen really tough men cracked
right up through illness – this is what is important, good health and
respect.

Respect is something that you also learn at Old Trafford. I think it
important that people should respect me because with respect comes

Carlo Sartori blazes in a shot, the latest Collyhurst recruit.

trust and without trust there is little hope of creating anything worth-while. Respect is something that starts right at the top with Manchester United. Everyone respects Sir Matt Busby, not just because he is the boss but as a man. As a young player I find him down to earth and straight with you. He has a gift for sorting out your problems, or at least he gets you thinking so you can see them straight.

If you have had a stinker, he is sympathetic but stern. He would never let sympathy sway his judgement, but at the same time you would know that he understands your position. This kind of situation is always cropping up in football of course where players are dropped and others promoted. One man's good fortune is another player's bad luck, and although a lot of players have been upset at times at Manchester United, as at all clubs, I don't think anyone has ever thought back afterwards and been really bitter.

I experienced these ups and downs of football for myself last season. In May, 1968, I thought I was sitting at the top of the football tree, celebrating my 19th birthday by scoring at Wembley to help Manchester United win the European Cup. It was an unforgettable experience. Yet a few months later I was dropped. I was upset and disappointed but I knew the boss was right and I think it was my confidence in knowing he was right that enabled me to win back my place, and, I hope, play a lot better.

I count myself lucky to have grown up in Collyhurst and finished my education, so to speak, at Old Trafford. I cannot think of myself at any other club. The bright lights don't appeal to me – either in London or even in Manchester. I suppose my pleasures are fairly simple.

There is nothing I like better than to come home, knowing there will always be a mug of tea, a clean shirt, and something to eat – like the cowheel pie I was telling you about! You couldn't count on that in every 'digs' and even if I got married one day these are the things I value and will be looking for.

I am ambitious in football of course, but my ambitions lie with Manchester United. I would like to play for England as well. I have had a few games with the Under-23 team and hope that one day Sir Alf Ramsey will give me another chance. I hope he knows I once gave up biting my nails to try and live up to an international image!

And if I did get back on the England scene with Nobby Stiles, it would be another feather in the cap for Collyhurst, which is something that would also give me a lot of pleasure.

111

Left: Pat Crerand with the European Cup and trainer Jack Crompton.

Our Man in Dublin

MANCHESTER UNITED'S coaching staff is second to none, but no matter how brilliant at developing young players, they are dependent in the first place on the quality of their raw material.

One of the richest sources of supply for Chief Scout Joe Armstrong at Old Trafford over the years has been the Republic of Ireland where the man in charge of sifting the wheat from the chaff is Billy Behan.

'Our man in Dublin' has been associated with the club for 34 years, first as a goalkeeper and now as resident scout whose first discovery was a truly great one. Let Billy Behan describe how United came to sign Johnny Carey – after missing another player!

'It was 1936. I had been looking after United's Irish interests since 1934, keeping them informed on our local scene even though English clubs at that time had no great interest in Irish players,' explains Behan.

'I wrote to Scott Duncan, then the manager at Old Trafford, about Benny Gaughran, centre-forward with Bohemians. Duncan came over to see for himself and was happy with what he saw.

'Arrangements were made to sign the player and for Louis Rocca, United's chief scout, to come over to complete the signing in November. But in the meantime, Glasgow Celtic's Dublin representative had stepped in with a better offer and while Rocca was travelling over to sign Gaughran, he was being shipped to Glasgow.'

So Louis Rocca arrived on a Saturday night to find Gaughran gone. Naturally he was bitterly disappointed, but the persuasive Behan asked him to have a look at another player the next day. He was a 17-year-old inside-left playing for St James' Gate against Cork. His name was Johnny Carey.

Back to Behan: 'Mr. Rocca agreed to have a look at the lad who was playing only his fifth game in the Free State League . . . and he scored

113

Tony Dunne comes in a long line of successful players from the Republic of Ireland, the work of Irish scout Billy Behan.

in the first minute although his side were eventually beaten 4–3.

'But the United chief scout had seen enough of Carey's talents and he wanted him straight away without any further reference to Old Trafford.'

Carey, of course, went on to become one of the Reds' greatest players, skippering them to Cup Final victory over Blackpool in that superb 1948 Wembley classic, leading his country in many internationals as well as the Rest of Europe against Great Britain in 1947. He was named Footballer of the Year in 1949.

Frank Swift, the late and great goalkeeper of Manchester City, once described Billy Whelan as: 'Master of the unexpected, brains of the attack and a player with fabulous footwork.'

Whelan joined United in April, 1953, another Behan discovery. United coach Bert Whalley, who died with Whelan in the Munich air crash, had crossed the Irish Sea to sign Whelan's Home Farm colleague, Vinny Ryan.

Says Behan: 'The club were urgently in need of an inside forward as replacement for the injured Jack Doherty for an F.A. Youth Cup final tie, a two-legged affair against Wolverhampton.

'And Ryan, normally a wing-half who had moved up to centre-forward to score a hat-trick in the Republic of Ireland's win over Luxembourg, was the target.

'But after Bert Whalley's arrival it became clear that prolonged negotiations would be necessary to clinch Ryan. So I immediately suggested that Whelan, whose natural position was inside forward, was the player United should have in the circumstances.'

Whelan was initially signed by United on amateur forms, but turned professional within a week and then nine days after his arrival played a star role in the Reds' blistering first leg Youth Cup final victory over Wolves.

He had come through the ranks at Home Farm starting as a 13-year-old and winning honours all along the way including schoolboy and youth international caps. But his first sporting medal was won . . . at hurling!

Behan recalls: 'Billy's school overlooked Dalymount Park, the big soccer ground in Dublin, but it was when helping his school that he first broke into the honours with a hurling trophy.

'Then it was on to Home Farm, undoubtedly one of the finest clubs in the world. It caters for some 17 boys' teams every week and the continued success of this organisation does not surprise me.'

Left: An elegant David Sadler arriving at Church for his wedding.

'At Old Trafford, however, Billy quickly made a big impression and after the Youth Cup success – Wolves were held 2–2 at Molineux – he went on the Reds' Continental and Irish tour in the summer of 1953. The following season, he was nursed along at third team level and then went on that fantastically successful tour of Switzerland and Germany when United's youths won ten out of 11 games, scoring 63 goals and conceeding only five.

'Whelan's outstanding performance on that tour was in a friendly match against a Bernese youth side at Burgdorf as a preliminary to the Switzerland v. Netherlands World Cup tie. He scored five great goals and so impressed the Brazilian World Cup squad who watched the game that their president approached Matt Busby asking if Whelan could go to South America. Somehow, he seemed surprised when the United manager said Whelan was not for sale . . . at any price.

'I remember travelling to London for the 1957 F.A. Cup final and talking about soccer with Matt Busby. And I recall Matt predicting that Billy Whelan and Bobby Charlton would prove the best inside-forwards in football, even greater than the great Hungarians, Ferenc Puskas and Alfredo Di Stefano.'

Alas that partnership was wrecked on an air strip at Munich.

Even as a ten-year-old, Johnny Giles had all the makings of a player-to-be in the eyes of Billy Behan who says:

'He was one of the most talented schoolboy players I have ever recruited for Old Trafford.'

'The highlight of his career came when he was a member of the United side that won the F.A. cup in 1963. When he moved to Leeds for a fee of £34,000 I was naturally sorry to see him leave Old Trafford, but he has done himself proud at Elland Road since and has built himself a distinguished career.'

In eight years at Old Trafford, Irishman Tony Dunne has scooped up a European Cup winners' medal, F.A. Cup winners' medal, two League Championship medals and a host of international caps. But unlike the other Behan discoveries, Dunne was a recognised player with a League of Ireland side and cost United a small fee when he was secured.

Says Behan: 'Although only little more than a boy when introduced to League of Ireland football, he had a polished assurance about his play which marked him as a player with a promising future. Even when with Shelbourne, his outstanding attribute and perhaps the key factor in his rise to greatness, was his fantastic speed off the mark and strong powers of recovery. I told Matt Busby I reckoned he was Old Trafford

117

material and well worth personal vetting.'

'Early in April, 1960, United played Shamrock Rovers in a friendly match – they were beaten 3–2 incidentally – and Matt decided to watch Rovers and Shelbourne in a League game the following Sunday. The grapevine had it that our target was Rovers' left back Pat Courtenay who had played a star role in the defeat of United a few days earlier.

'You can imagine how I felt when Tony had his hand ripped open by studs which left him with his arm bandaged to his side throughout the second half. But I need not have worried. After the match Matt turned and said: "I've seen enough of him. He'll make the grade all right."

'So terms with Shelbourne were quickly agreed. The fee was £5,000 with a further £500 to be paid when Tony played ten League games and a further £500 when he gained his first international cap.

John Fitzpatrick played in six different positions for United last season. He had a successful run at right-back and in this match against Arsenal he was an airborne inside-right challenging goalkeeper Bob Wilson (left) and Frank McLintock.

'When we went to discuss terms with Tony he had disappeared! He had gone to the pictures with his girl friend Ann, now his wife, and it was near midnight before the signing was completed.'

Tony went with United's youths on a summer tour, started the following season in the reserves but within two months was in the first team making his debut against Burnley at Turf Moor. The trail to the top had started for yet another of Behan's finds.

And Billy Behan is still working hard on United's behalf in Ireland. Two more of his discoveries are currently thrusting their way up through the reserves. Mike Kelly is a winger from Ireland whose main claim to sporting fame was as fly-half in his college rugby team, while Donal Givens was top scorer in last season's Central League team.

Scouts like Billy Behan provide the lifeblood for Manchester United's continued success.

Carlo Sartori was at outside-right in this League clash with Leeds United at Elland Road.

How It All Starts

THOUSANDS of soccer-mad youngsters would probably give their eye-teeth to line up alongside the likes of Bobby Charlton, Denis Law and George Best. For a few, the dream DOES come true.

United and all the other professional League clubs are geared to finding the right recruits. The bigger the club, the wider the net will be cast. The last chapter spotlighted the Republic of Ireland, one of Old Trafford's most productive hunting grounds, and as I described earlier, Collyhurst has also done United proud.

Manchester United's scouting team is headed by Joe Armstrong, 75 this year. Behind him are two scouts in Scotland and two in Ireland, while there is a man in the North-East, and two more, including Joe Armstrong, Jnr., who help with the club's scouting activities locally.

Between them they aim to ensure United have their share of the cream of the country's footballing talent. This was the pattern laid down when Sir Matt Busby first stepped into management and began to set the pace in the production of youthful talent.

Like Matt Busby, Joe Armstrong has been with both United and Manchester City. He scouted for the Maine Road club before the war and then switched to Old Trafford soon after Matt's appointment as manager in 1946. He was also a Post Office engineer, scouting in his spare time and at weekends. He became resident chief scout with United at the age of 65 when most people are preparing to knock off work and put their feet up.

As a tribute to the man who only took up a full-time soccer post when he 'retired' – if that doesn't sound too Irish – Sir Matt took Joe with the team for the big European Cup-tie against Rapid Vienna in Austria. It was the first time he had tasted the glamour of the European scene for such an important match and seen the results of his shrewd

Right: Denis Law, in action here against Arsenal, is the kind of star schoolboys would give their eye teeth to line up alongside.

judgement and eye for assessing youngsters blossoming at the highest and most testing level.

'I appreciate the gesture,' said Joe at the time. But I suspect it was also a trip that left him with mixed feelings for while he was away, his present youngsters were playing an F.A. Youth Cup-tie against Everton.

It was the first Youth Cup match, home or away, he had missed for 15 years!

Star-struck boys and football fond parents write to Matt Busby in their thousands asking for a trial. But the odds are that if they really have talent they will already be on someone or other's books.

The passport to a major club like United is a place in the England schoolboy team or to get somewhere near like the final trial between the North and the South, or perhaps to appear a little lower down the scale and play for a county, local town or city team.

By the time a boy has reached international level he will probably already be on a club's books as an 'associated schoolboy'. This gives a club first claim on a boy should he decide to take up football as a career when he leaves school.

The system was introduced a few years ago to prevent a boy being unduly pestered by rival clubs over a long period, for of course once he has signed for one, the others are automatically barred from approaching him. The scheme also allows clubs to invite their boys down for training and coaching to the mutual advantage of both sides.

Competition for the most promising boys is intense as more and more clubs come to appreciate that creating their own players is cheaper than buying them at anything up to £100,000. The result is that some schoolboys are being signed as early as 13, though this is not such a gamble to a professional soccer scout as it sounds, for skill shows through even at that tender age.

Unless they elect to remain amateurs, the boys leave school to become apprentice professionals between the ages of 15 and 17 and great care is taken with these embryo footballers.

Let's look at the 15-year-old boys who reported at Old Trafford last season as brand-new apprentice professionals. They included three of the England schoolboy team . . . Eric Young an inside-forward who comes from the North-East, Kevin Lewis a centre-half from Hull, son of a fisherman, and Tommy O'Neil a wing-half from St. Helens, Lancashire, who was also a schoolboy international at Rugby League.

More boys, like Manchester's Tony Young, left school during the year and joined the apprentices as starlets in training for the team of the

123

Bobby Charlton is club captain, and also a dashing cricketer as he showed when United lined up against Manchester City at the other Old Trafford.

Nobby Stiles also in studious mood and voted one of the best bespectacled men in the country.

future, because recruiting is a process that never ceases.

What kind of life do they lead?

They spend most mornings and afternoons at United's training centre, The Cliff, in Salford, which has a big indoor playing pitch as well as an outdoor ground. There, under the direct supervision of trainer Jack Crompton, and for six years his assistant Wilf McGuinness along with coach John Aston, they learn more of the arts of the game.

Left: A few players keep on their studies, like Alan Gowling reading economics at Manchester University.

Sir Matt Busby keeps a more distant but nevertheless watchful eye on their progress while his assistant, Jimmy Murphy, concentrates on the youthful stream.

The boys are not coddled because of course professional football is no job for a 'softy'. They have menial tasks like cleaning boots and mopping up dressing rooms to perform as well as kicking a football about. Character building is perhaps as important as skill and there is equally no room for a 'big-head'.

United, of course, have had startling success with their youth scheme. For instance only two of the team that won the European Cup in 1968 were signed for big fees: the remainder like Bobby Charlton, George Best and Nobby Stiles all graduated through the junior A and B teams for which the apprentices play to round off their week's training.

The club's care does not stop with the training of course. All the boys who come from away go into specially selected 'digs'. Some of these landladies in the vicinity of Old Trafford have been taking in players for years.

There is Mrs. Dormant of Gorse Avenue for instance who used to look after Duncan Edwards and now has Jimmy Hall from Belfast and Mel Simmonds from Reading. Mrs. Cropper of Sutherland Road has a houseful, Don Givens who comes from Dublin, Steve James from Wolverhampton and Laurie Millerchip of Coventry.

Mrs. Barratt of South Lonsdale Street looks after Peter O'Sullivan whose home is at Colwyn Bay and Francis Burns who comes from Glasgow. Francis has been in club digs for five years since he left St. Augustins' School at Coatbridge. Until he became a full professional at 17 the club paid for his keep and he says: 'All the lads are well fed and the club are always in touch with our landladies to check what time we come in at night and make sure we are behaving ourselves. It is a good thing of course, because 15 is not very old to leave home for some boys and we need a bit of looking after at times.'

They are more mothers than landladies of course. George Best was homesick and went back to Belfast after two days in Manchester. But Mrs. Fullaway of Aycliff Avenue soon cured that when George was persuaded to return. Since then she has had to cope with all kinds of problems like asking the swinging George to get rid of some of his clothes because they just did not have enough room to put them.

Mrs. Fullaway is certainly more of a mother than a landlady. When she lost one of her 'lodgers', she was guest of honour at his wedding! David Sadler asked her to accept a gift in front of all the other guests

George Best, a star to inspire all soccer-mad youngsters.

at the reception and paid tribute to the way he had been looked after. In fact he said he was glad his new wife, Christine, had been given a cookery book because he had been rather spoiled by his landlady.

This is the kind of atmosphere created by United's dozen or so landladies who contribute their vital back-room role towards producing the soccer stars of tomorrow.